INTRODUCING
ISSUES WITH
OPPOSING
VIEWPOINTS®

The Taliban

Lauri S. Scherer, *Book Editor*

GREENHAVEN PRESS
A part of Gale, Cengage Learning

GALE
CENGAGE Learning·

Detroit • New York • San Francisco • New Haven, Conn • Waterville, Maine • London

Elizabeth Des Chenes, *Director, Publishing Solutions*

© 2013 Greenhaven Press, a part of Gale, Cengage Learning

Gale and Greenhaven Press are registered trademarks used herein under license.

For more information, contact:
Greenhaven Press
27500 Drake Rd.
Farmington Hills, MI 48331-3535
Or you can visit our Internet site at gale.cengage.com

For product information and technology assistance, contact us at

Gale Customer Support, 1-800-877-4253
For permission to use material from this text or product, submit all requests online at www.cengage.com/permissions

Further permissions questions can be e-mailed to permissionrequest@cengage.com

Articles in Greenhaven Press anthologies are often edited for length to meet page requirements. In addition, original titles of these works are changed to clearly present the main thesis and to explicitly indicate the author's opinion. Every effort is made to ensure that Greenhaven Press accurately reflects the original intent of the authors. Every effort has been made to trace the owners of copyrighted material.

Cover image © Oleg Zabielin/Shutterstock.com.

LIBRARY OF CONGRESS CATALOGING-IN-PUBLICATION DATA

The Taliban / Lauri S. Scherer, book editor.
    p. cm. -- (Introducing issues with opposing viewpoints)
    Includes bibliographical references and index.
    ISBN 978-0-7377-6283-9 (hbk.)
  1. Taliban--Juvenile literature. 2. Afghanistan--History--1989-2001--Juvenile literature.
3. Afghanistan--History--2001---Juvenile literature. 4. Afghan War, 2001---Juvenile
literature. I. Scherer, Lauri S.
    DS371.3.T3262 2013
    958.104'7--dc23

                         2012036358

Printed in the United States of America
1 2 3 4 5 6 7 16 15 14 13 12

Contents

Foreword

Indulging in a wide spectrum of ideas, beliefs, and perspectives is a critical cornerstone of democracy. After all, it is often debates over differences of opinion, such as whether to legalize abortion, how to treat prisoners, or when to enact the death penalty, that shape our society and drive it forward. Such diversity of thought is frequently regarded as the hallmark of a healthy and civilized culture. As the Reverend Clifford Schutjer of the First Congregational Church in Mansfield, Ohio, declared in a 2001 sermon, "Surrounding oneself with only like-minded people, restricting what we listen to or read only to what we find agreeable is irresponsible. Refusing to entertain doubts once we make up our minds is a subtle but deadly form of arrogance." With this advice in mind, Introducing Issues with Opposing Viewpoints books aim to open readers' minds to the critically divergent views that comprise our world's most important debates.

Introducing Issues with Opposing Viewpoints simplifies for students the enormous and often overwhelming mass of material now available via print and electronic media. Collected in every volume is an array of opinions that captures the essence of a particular controversy or topic. Introducing Issues with Opposing Viewpoints books embody the spirit of nineteenth-century journalist Charles A. Dana's axiom: "Fight for your opinions, but do not believe that they contain the whole truth, or the only truth." Absorbing such contrasting opinions teaches students to analyze the strength of an argument and compare it to its opposition. From this process readers can inform and strengthen their own opinions, or be exposed to new information that will change their minds. Introducing Issues with Opposing Viewpoints is a mosaic of different voices. The authors are statesmen, pundits, academics, journalists, corporations, and ordinary people who have felt compelled to share their experiences and ideas in a public forum. Their words have been collected from newspapers, journals, books, speeches, interviews, and the Internet, the fastest growing body of opinionated material in the world.

Introducing Issues with Opposing Viewpoints shares many of the well-known features of its critically acclaimed parent series, Opposing Viewpoints. The articles are presented in a pro/con format, allowing readers to absorb divergent perspectives side by side. Active reading questions preface each viewpoint, requiring the student to approach the material thoughtfully and carefully. Useful charts, graphs, and cartoons supplement each article. A thorough introduction provides readers with crucial background on an issue. An annotated bibliography points the reader toward articles, books, and websites that contain additional information on the topic. An appendix of organizations to contact contains a wide variety of charities, nonprofit organizations, political groups, and private enterprises that each hold a position on the issue at hand. Finally, a comprehensive index allows readers to locate content quickly and efficiently.

Introducing Issues with Opposing Viewpoints is also significantly different from Opposing Viewpoints. As the series title implies, its presentation will help introduce students to the concept of opposing viewpoints and learn to use this material to aid in critical writing and debate. The series' four-color, accessible format makes the books attractive and inviting to readers of all levels. In addition, each viewpoint has been carefully edited to maximize a reader's understanding of the content. Short but thorough viewpoints capture the essence of an argument. A substantial, thought-provoking essay question placed at the end of each viewpoint asks the student to further investigate the issues raised in the viewpoint, compare and contrast two authors' arguments, or consider how one might go about forming an opinion on the topic at hand. Each viewpoint contains sidebars that include at-a-glance information and handy statistics. A Facts About section located in the back of the book further supplies students with relevant facts and figures.

Following in the tradition of the Opposing Viewpoints series, Greenhaven Press continues to provide readers with invaluable exposure to the controversial issues that shape our world. As John Stuart Mill once wrote: "The only way in which a human being can make some approach to knowing the whole of a subject is by hearing what can be said about it by persons of every variety of opinion and studying all modes in which it can be looked at by every character of mind. No wise man ever acquired his wisdom in any mode but this." It is to this principle that Introducing Issues with Opposing Viewpoints books are dedicated.

Introduction

The Taliban were originally a group of Islamic fundamentalists who took control of Afghanistan in the mid-1990s after the nation was left lawless and ruined by decades of foreign invasion and civil war. Primarily composed of Afghan refugees who spent the 1980s and early 1990s in Pakistan's religious schools, the Taliban (which literally means "students") began gaining control of Afghan areas in 1994, and by 1996, about two-thirds of the country, including its capital, was firmly under their control.

The second half of the twentieth century had not been good to Afghanistan: Multiple coups in the 1970s eventually led to an invasion by the Soviet Union in 1979, which wreaked havoc on the nation until the former superpower's withdrawal in 1989. Even then, weak leadership resulted in a civil war from 1992 to 1996, which further devastated the country. Thus, the Taliban's takeover was in part welcome, because it was the first time in decades Afghanistan had firm and authoritative leaders.

Yet this leadership came at enormous social cost. Over the course of their rule, the Taliban imposed many draconian laws on the population, ranging from bans on women's education and rights, e.g., forcing them to leave their homes only in the company of a male escort, prohibiting kite flying, owning pet birds, and listening to music, all of which were deemed un-Islamic. Furthermore, the Taliban doled out medieval punishments like stoning and amputation for infractions such as having sex outside of marriage or shoplifting. For these reasons, most other countries viewed the Taliban as an extreme, backward, and threatening group.

Mullah Muhammad Omar, the leader of this group, found a like-minded companion in Saudi national Osama bin Laden, who came to Afghanistan in 1996. Bin Laden had formed a group known as al Qaeda (literally, "The Base"), which promoted an Islamist, anti-Western ideology and used terrorist methods to advance its goals. Bin Laden sought a place where he could develop his beliefs, train followers, and plot terrorist attacks. Afghanistan was a natural choice: He had a prior relationship with the country (as a younger man, he had fought in Afghanistan against the Soviets), and the Taliban shared his extremist view of Islam and hatred of the West. The Taliban agreed to let him operate unfettered within their country. From this safe haven, Bin Laden planned several terrorist attacks against the United States, including the 1998 bombings of US embassies in Kenya and Tanzania and the 2000 bombing of the USS *Cole*, a ship that was stationed in Yemen.

By 2001 the United States was fed up with the Taliban's tolerance of Bin Laden. In fact, on July 4, 1999, President Bill Clinton declared a national emergency about the "unusual and extraordinary threat" posed by the Taliban. "I have exercised my statutory authority to declare a National emergency with respect to the threat to the United States posed by the actions and policies of the Afghan Taliban," wrote Clinton in a letter to representatives of the US House of Representatives and the Senate. "The Taliban continues to provide safe haven to Usama bin Ladin allowing him and the Al-Qaida organization to operate from Taliban-controlled territory a network of terrorist training camps and to use Afghanistan as a base from which to sponsor terrorist operations against the United States."[1]

The United States imposed sanctions on the Taliban and conducted missile strikes on areas of Afghanistan to try to oust Bin Laden. None worked, and so the next, and worst, al Qaeda–sponsored terrorist attack was carried out: On September 11, 2001, nineteen al Qaeda–trained terrorists hijacked four airplanes and flew them into buildings and other areas inside the United States, killing nearly three thousand Americans. It was immediately clear that Bin Laden bore responsibility for masterminding the attacks, and the United States demanded that the Taliban hand him over to face justice. The Taliban refused, so the United States— along with troops from dozens of other countries—invaded Afghanistan in October 2001, quickly removing the Taliban from power.

Though ousted, the Taliban were not defeated. Many suspected Taliban were captured in the early years of the war, but over the next decade, surviving and new Taliban members conducted a persistent insurgency, attacking US and international troops, Afghan government officials, international embassies, and other targets wherever they were able. By 2009 Taliban forces had gained control of critical areas of the country; by 2012 the Taliban remained so integral to Afghanistan's future that the United States was considering engaging high-level members in peace negotiations.

It is important to understand that the Taliban that in the 1990s sheltered Bin Laden (who was finally killed by US forces in Pakistan in May 2011) are very different than the group that vies for control of Afghanistan today. Today's Taliban comprise multiple groups with varied interests, goals, and histories. As historian Juan Cole has put it, "What we're calling the Taliban, it's actually a misnomer. There are, like, five different groups that we're swooping up and calling [themselves] the Taliban."[2]

Some of the modern Taliban stem from the original group. Several original and senior Taliban members—like Mullah Omar—remain alive, though US officials believe they operate from nearby Pakistan. Those with ties to the original Taliban are often associated with attacks in southern parts of the country, where they have the most authority with locals.

Also active under the Taliban umbrella is a group called Hizb-e-Islami, which was formed by an Afghan warlord in the 1970s. Hizb-e-Islami joined forces with the Taliban after the 2001 American invasion and is responsible for many of the insurgent attacks that today occur in the northern areas of the country. Hizb-e-Islami may have also infiltrated Afghan police and government.

Then there are members of the Haqqani network, who operate sometimes with the Taliban and Hizb-e-Islami and sometimes on their own. Members of the Haqqani network have conducted some of the boldest and most deadly insurgent attacks to date. They have tried to assassinate President Hamid Karzai multiple times and also were behind a serious assault on Kabul in September 2011.

In addition to the Haqqani network, Hizb-e-Islami, and the original Taliban members, various warlords, drug cartels, and other criminal organizations are also active in the nation, either conducting their own insurgent campaigns or joining with other groups to do so. Still other groups from Pakistan carry out attacks in the area, for reasons related to the drug trade, politics, power struggles, religion, and more.

The diversity of these groups explains why the Taliban are so difficult to fight. Who composes the Taliban, what they want, and how they operate are among the many issues discussed in *Introducing Issues with Opposing Viewpoints: The Taliban*. Pro/con article pairs expose readers to the basic debates surrounding the identity of the Taliban;

how strong they are; the threat they pose to Afghanistan and the United States; how they are funded; and, perhaps most importantly, how the United States should deal with them to end the war and stabilize Afghanistan.

Notes
1. Quoted in *Middle East Quarterly*, "It's Official: Taliban Pose a Danger to the United States," September 1999, pp. 92–93. http://www.meforum.org/483/its-official-taliban-pose-a-danger-to-the-united.
2. Quoted in Public Broadcasting Service, *Bill Moyers Journal*, May 15, 2009. www.pbs.org/moyers/journal/05152009/transcript4.html.

Chapter 1

How Powerful Are the Taliban?

Taliban members patrol their stronghold in a Pakistani tribal region along the Afghan border. Just how much of a threat the Taliban pose is the subject of debate.

The Taliban Pose a Significant Threat

Louie Gohmert and Dana Rohrabacher

"Leaving Afghanistan to the same terrorist thugs who enabled the September 11th attacks is the very definition of insanity."

Louie Gohmert is a Republican who represents the state of Texas in the US House of Representatives, where Republican Dana Rohrabacher represents the state of California. In the following viewpoint they argue that the Taliban pose a significant threat to peace in Afghanistan, to US soldiers fighting there, and to Americans at home. They remind readers that the Taliban gave refuge to former al Qaeda leader Osama bin Laden, allowing him to plan the September 11 attacks from Afghanistan. Gohmert and Rohrabacher say the Taliban would not hesitate to shelter other terrorists. They fight brutally against US soldiers stationed in Afghanistan, and carry out gruesome attacks on other Afghans. Gohmert and Rohrabacher conclude that the Taliban cannot be trusted and that the United States must not be tempted to view them as partners in peace.

AS YOU READ, CONSIDER THE FOLLOWING QUESTIONS:
1. How did the Taliban treat former Afghan president Burhanuddin Rabbani, according to the authors?
2. What is an IED, and how does it factor into the authors' argument?
3. What percentage of US Agency for International Development (USAID) money do Gohmert and Rohrabacher say ends up in Taliban-controlled areas of Afghanistan?

I n September 2011 Former President Burhanuddin Rabbani, a key Northern Alliance[1] leader and the only Tajik to be President of Afghanistan, was murdered after Taliban emissaries promised to deliver him an important message of peace. When welcomed, they blew him up.

In August 2011, after a conspiracy that lured in members of our Seal Team Six[2] with other heroic Americans, the Taliban set up an ambush and murdered them.

The Taliban Cannot Be Trusted

Following those brutal attacks, President Barack Obama's strategy has been to hasten negotiations with the Taliban. Additionally, the Obama administration has now not only offered to release known Taliban terrorists from detention, but has already released some and additionally offered to legitimize our sworn enemy by furnishing them a princely office in Qatar.

In return, Obama's agents defend that they are being tough on the Taliban by demanding that they not use the office to raise funds to support their terrorism. That is a bit reminiscent of the [US president Bill] Clinton–[secretary of state Madeleine] Albright demand of North Korea that if we give them nuclear technology, they must promise to use it for electric generation and not weapons.

1. The Northern Alliance was an anti-Taliban group in Afghanistan that sided with US invasion forces.
2. Members of this same SEAL (Sea, Air, and Land) team killed al Qaeda terrorist leader Osama bin Laden in May 2011.

Texas congressman Louie Gohmert believes that the Taliban cannot be trusted to negotiate faithfully and that the United States should not be tempted to view them as a partner in peace.

The Taliban Have Grown Stronger

According to many Afghans, all of these and other Obama Administration actions give substantial credence to the Taliban claim, supported privately by some Pakistani leaders, that the U.S. has lost in Afghanistan and is now begging them for negotiations. One Taliban leader who was released from detention by the Obama administration for medical and end of life purposes, is now back in command and recently demanded on Afghan TV that since the Americans have now lost and are begging for negotiations, Afghans disloyal to the Taliban must come ask forgiveness and for safety from the Taliban.

A Northern Alliance leader says that of the more than 800 Taliban detainees that have been released, he is now seeing many of them fighting, killing and terrorizing again. Yet, the Northern Alliance leaders are being effectively shut out of the plans for the way forward, while being demonized by the American government they helped.

The State Department even went to extraordinary lengths to attempt preventing the writers from meeting with the Northern Alliance leaders. We were able to meet, with some help from foreign friends, but clearly the Obama administration and its comrades mean for our allies to stay under the bus when they throw them there.

U.S. Mismanagement Has Helped the Taliban

In late 2001–2002, the Taliban were defeated with less than 500 Americans embedded with the Northern Alliance, but now [in 2012] the Taliban is stronger while we have more than 100,000 American troops in Afghanistan. Though Vice-President [Joe] Biden says the Taliban are not our enemies, American soldiers in Afghanistan say the Taliban are still creating IED's [improvised explosive devices], firing bullets, firing rockets and doing all they can to kill Americans, so it seemed to them that the Taliban certainly think they are our enemy. This points straight to the fact our military is not the problem; it's their commander in chief who is the current weak link in our chain of command.

> **FAST FACT**
>
> On April 15, 2012, Taliban insurgents carried out deadly and coordinated attacks on military bases, government buildings, and embassies throughout Afghanistan. It was the group's largest and most organized attack in eleven years.

To date, the U.S. nation-building experiment in Afghanistan has produced instability, violence, skyrocketing drug production, widespread corruption, fraudulently rigged elections and the general disapproval of this new government by its own people. Under the U.S.-approved, Afghan Constitution, President [Hamid] Karzai appoints all governors for the provinces, all mayors, police chiefs, the slate for one third of the Senate candidates, and even a segment of the Class 1 teachers in the country. He even has power of the purse that the U.S. President does not have. Clearly this is a formula for heightened corruption, while isolating and ignoring many ethnic groups that make up the very essence of Afghan society.

Corrupt Officials Are Getting Rich

Many with first-hand experience fighting the Taliban say they are dependent on Pakistan for their marching orders, strategy, and weaponry. In the meantime, President Karzai's regime has dropped every pretense of appreciation for American sacrifice in blood and treasure as demonstrated by his recent threats to align with Pakistan, Iran and China even as we continue to prop up his government. From Karzai's perspective, he may well see the Taliban and Pakistan as holding his fate in their hands once the U.S. pulls out.

At the same time, the U.S. is pouring billions of dollars into Afghanistan that comprises the largest portion of the Afghan government's own budget. U.S.A.I.D. [US Agency for International Development] alone is pouring $3.6 billion a year into the country for aid and projects while the money often fails to get past corrupt government officials with 80 percent going to Taliban areas and a tiny fraction going to areas where our allies reside.

The Afghan leaders have become increasingly enriched as their contempt for us has continued to grow. At President Karzai's encouragement, we have politically and militarily undermined the natural and historic barrier to the Taliban, which is the non-Pashtun peoples of the North, Central and Western parts of Afghanistan. As these non-Pashtun communities were weakened, their leaders were undermined by U.S. support for Karzai and his concentration of power.

The Way Forward

The critical next step should be to insist on a new Constitutional Loya Jirga, or convention, that will draft a new constitution enshrining federalism as the new form of government. This would break

Americans Think the Taliban Threaten National Security

A poll taken jointly by NBC News and the *Wall Street Journal* found that most Americans think the Taliban pose a serious threat to national security.

Question: If the Taliban returned to power in Afghanistan, how much of a threat do you think this would be to American national security?

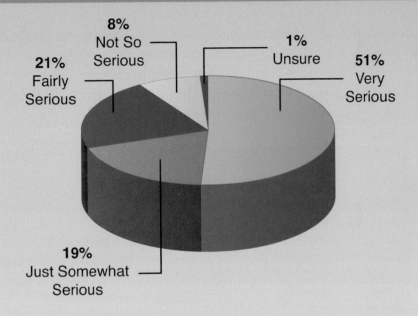

8%
Not So
Serious

1%
Unsure

21%
Fairly
Serious

51%
Very
Serious

19%
Just Somewhat
Serious

Taken from: NBC News/*Wall Street Journal*, August 5–9, 2010.

the Taliban's ability to dominate Afghanistan by strengthening those communities opposed to the return of the Taliban and their Al-Qaeda allies. It would give Afghans the kind of hope that our founders provided Americans 225 years ago with our Constitution.

We should insist on local elections of Afghan governors and mayors who may then select the police chiefs. Electing regional leaders would serve to eliminate the conduit of corruption built into the present system, while at the same time giving the governing authority back to the people who are now being disenfranchised.

This course would establish the basis for a political system that allows each of Afghanistan's ethnic communities to retain their identity and protect them from the Taliban's violent ethnic repression, brutality and regressive domination. The resulting political framework would also enable trust and goodwill to be built between Afghanistan's diverse communities as each community would have a direct and important say in its own future.

The Taliban Are Terrorist Thugs

Perhaps we should even consider support for a Balochistan [province] carved out of Pakistan to diminish radical power there also. Surely, leaving Afghanistan to the same terrorist thugs who enabled the September 11th attacks is the very definition of insanity. The way forward should not include the current Obama plan of putting our future in Taliban hands that are covered with American blood.

> **EVALUATING THE AUTHOR'S ARGUMENTS:**
>
> **Louie Gohmert and Dana Rohrabacher argue that the Taliban are dangerous because they could again shelter terrorists like Osama bin Laden, whose al Qaeda group carried out the September 11 attacks. How would John Mueller, author of the following viewpoint, respond to this claim?**

The Threat from the Taliban Has Been Exaggerated

John Mueller

"If [the Taliban] came to power again now, they would be highly unlikely to host provocative terrorist groups whose actions could lead to another outside intervention."

The Taliban do not pose a severe threat to the American people, argues John Mueller in the following viewpoint. He says contrary to conventional wisdom, the Taliban did not play a significant role in the September 11 attacks. Relations between the Taliban and al Qaeda were weak at that point, and evidence shows that the attacks were not even plotted from inside Afghanistan. Mueller says that even if the Taliban came to power again in Afghanistan, they probably would not provide safe haven to any terrorist groups because it would provoke another war against them. He acknowledges that the Taliban would likely be brutal rulers of Afghanistan but says this is not a sufficient reason for the United States to be at war there. Mueller concludes that the Taliban do not pose enough of a threat to the American people to justify the ongoing war effort.

Mueller is a political science professor at Ohio State University.

AS YOU READ, CONSIDER THE FOLLOWING QUESTIONS:
1. Describe the Taliban's relationship with the terrorist group al Qaeda in the 1990s, according to Mueller.
2. What involvement does the author say the Taliban had in the September 11 terrorist attacks?
3. What kind of effort are Americans unlikely to want to sacrifice soldiers' lives for, according to Mueller?

[Former president] George W. Bush led the United States into war in Iraq on the grounds that [former Iraqi dictator] Saddam Hussein might give his country's nonexistent weapons of mass destruction to terrorists. Now, Bush's successor is perpetuating the war in Afghanistan with comparably dubious arguments about the danger posed by the Taliban and al Qaeda.

The Truth About the Taliban

President Barack Obama insists that the U.S. mission in Afghanistan is about "making sure that al Qaeda cannot attack the U.S. homeland and U.S. interests and our allies" or "project violence against" American citizens. The reasoning is that if the Taliban win in Afghanistan, al Qaeda will once again be able to set up shop there to carry out its dirty work. As the president puts it, Afghanistan would "again be a base for terrorists who want to kill as many of our people as they possibly can." This argument is constantly repeated but rarely examined; given the costs and risks associated with the Obama administration's plans for the region, it is time such statements be given the scrutiny they deserve.

Multiple sources, including Lawrence Wright's book *The Looming Tower*, make clear that the Taliban was a reluctant host to al Qaeda in the 1990s and felt betrayed when the terrorist group repeatedly violated agreements to refrain from issuing inflammatory statements and fomenting violence abroad. Then the al Qaeda-sponsored 9/11 attacks—which the Taliban had nothing to do with—led to the toppling of the Taliban's regime. Given the Taliban's limited interest in issues outside the "AfPak" region [including Afghanistan and Pakistan], if they came to power again now, they would be highly unlikely to host provocative terrorist groups whose actions could lead to another outside intervention. And even if al Qaeda were able to relocate to Afghanistan after a Taliban victory there, it would still have to operate under the same siege situation it presently enjoys in what Obama calls its "safe haven" in Pakistan.

A Questionable Notion

The very notion that al Qaeda needs a secure geographic base to carry out its terrorist operations, moreover, is questionable. After all, the operational base for 9/11 was in Hamburg, Germany. Conspiracies involving small numbers of people require communication, money, and planning—but not a major protected base camp.

President Barack Obama has stressed that if the Taliban returned to power in Afghanistan the Afghan people would be subject "to brutal governance, international isolation, a paralyzed economy, and the denial of basic human rights."

At present, al Qaeda consists of a few hundred people running around in Pakistan, seeking to avoid detection and helping the Taliban when possible. It also has a disjointed network of fellow travelers around the globe who communicate over the Internet. Over the last decade, the group has almost completely discredited itself in the Muslim world due to the fallout from the 9/11 attacks and subsequent counterproductive terrorism, much of it directed against Muslims. No convincing evidence has been offered publicly to show that al Qaeda Central has put together a single full operation anywhere in the world since 9/11. And, outside of war zones, the violence perpetrated by al Qaeda affiliates, wannabes, and lookalikes combined has resulted in the deaths of some 200 to 300 people per year, and may be declining. That is 200 to 300 too many, of course, but it scarcely suggests that "the safety of people around the world is at stake," as Obama dramatically puts it.

In addition, al Qaeda has yet to establish a significant presence in the United States. In 2002, U.S. intelligence reports asserted that the number of trained al Qaeda operatives in the United States was between 2,000 and 5,000, and FBI Director Robert Mueller assured a Senate committee that al Qaeda had "developed a support infrastructure" in the country and achieved both "the ability and the intent to inflict significant casualties in the U.S. with little warning." However, after years of well funded sleuthing, the FBI and other investigative agencies have been unable to uncover a single true al Qaeda sleeper cell or operative within the country. Mueller's

FAST FACT

In January 2012 the Taliban opened an office in Qatar (a country on the Arabian Peninsula), where it intended to conduct diplomatic operations.

rallying cry has now been reduced to a comparatively bland formulation: "We believe al Qaeda is still seeking to infiltrate operatives into the U.S. from overseas."

"Small, Lethal, and Disjointed"

Even that may not be true. Since 9/11, some two million foreigners have been admitted to the United States legally and many others, of

Americans Think the United States Should Leave Afghanistan Immediately

A 2012 poll taken by the Pew Research Center found the majority of Americans think US troops should be removed from Afghanistan immediately, indicating that they have grown weary of the war and think the Taliban pose less of a threat than they did in years past.

Question: "Do you think the United States should keep military troops in Afghanistan until the situation has stabilized, or do you think the United States should remove troops as soon as possible?"

Date	Stay Until Stabilized %	Remove Troops as Soon as Possible %	Unsure %
April 4–5, 2012	32	57	8
May 5–8, 2011	43	49	8
June 16–20, 2010	53	40	6
Feb. 20–24, 2008	61	32	7

Taken from: Pew Research Center, April 4–15, 2012.

course, have entered illegally. Even if border security has been so effective that 90 percent of al Qaeda's operatives have been turned away or deterred from entering the United States, some should have made it in—and some of those, it seems reasonable to suggest, would have been picked up by law enforcement by now. The lack of attacks inside the United States combined with the inability of the FBI to find any potential attackers suggests that the terrorists are either not trying very hard or are far less clever and capable than usually depicted.

Policymakers and the public at large should keep in mind the words of Glenn Carle, a 23 year veteran of the CIA who served as deputy national intelligence officer for transnational threats: "We must see jihadists for the small, lethal, disjointed and miserable opponents that they are." Al Qaeda "has only a handful of individuals capable of planning, organizing and leading a terrorist operation," Carle notes, and "its capabilities are far inferior to its desires."

"A Weak Reed"

President Obama has said that there is also a humanitarian element to the Afghanistan mission. A return of the Taliban, he points out, would condemn the Afghan people "to brutal governance, international isolation, a paralyzed economy, and the denial of basic human rights." This concern is legitimate—the Afghan people appear to be quite strongly opposed to a return of the Taliban, and they are surely entitled to some peace after 30 years of almost continual warfare, much of it imposed on them from outside.

The problem, as Obama is doubtlessly well aware, is that Americans are far less willing to sacrifice lives for missions that are essentially humanitarian than for those that seek to deal with a threat directed at the United States itself. People who embrace the idea of a humanitarian mission will continue to support Obama's policy in Afghanistan—at least if they think it has a chance of success—but many Americans (and Europeans) will increasingly start to question how many lives such a mission is worth.

This questioning, in fact, is well under way. Because of its ties to 9/11, the war in Afghanistan has enjoyed considerably greater public support than the war in Iraq did (or, for that matter, the wars in Korea or Vietnam). However, there has been a considerable dropoff in that support of late. If Obama's national security justification for his war in Afghanistan comes to seem as spurious as Bush's national security justification for his war in Iraq, he, like Bush will increasingly have only the humanitarian argument to fall back on. And that is likely to be a weak reed.

> **EVALUATING THE AUTHOR'S ARGUMENTS:**
>
> John Mueller acknowledges that if the Taliban were to again rule Afghanistan, they would likely violate Afghans' human rights. Yet he says most Americans would not think this a good enough reason for the United States to carry on a war. What do you think? Are humanitarian causes worth sacrificing soldiers' lives? Or should wars only be waged when the lives of Americans are directly threatened? Explain your reasoning and where you stand on this issue.

Viewpoint

3

US Troop Presence in Afghanistan Keeps the Taliban Weak

"The only way [the Taliban and others] will shoot their way back into power is if we abandon the vast majority of Afghans."

Max Boot

Supporting Afghanistan financially and with troop presence is the only way to keep the Taliban weak, argues Max Boot in the following viewpoint. He says the Taliban and other insurgents that operate in the country are barely strong enough to pull off a devastating attack. In most places, Afghans are getting back to a normal, peaceful existence after years of war. But Boot warns this will all be undone should American troops leave the country. He warns that the Taliban will come out of hiding to fill in the spaces left behind by troops. He thinks the Afghans need help to keep their large and volatile country stable, so Boot suggests that the United States and its allies be prepared to commit troops and funds for years to come, lest the gains made over the last decade of war be erased.

Boot is a senior fellow at the Council on Foreign Relations.

AS YOU READ, CONSIDER THE FOLLOWING QUESTIONS:
1. What was the outcome of an April 2012 insurgent attack on NATO forces, according to the author?
2. How many troops does Boot think the United States should maintain in Afghanistan through 2014?
3. What kinds of activities and skills do Afghan troops need help with, according to Boot?

The Tet Offensive[1] it wasn't. On Sunday [April 15, 2012], insurgents belonging to the Haqqani network [an insurgent group] attacked seven high-profile sites in Kabul and other parts of Afghanistan. The Afghan National Security Forces responded swiftly and professionally with minimal assistance from NATO [North Atlantic Treaty Organization]. Far more insurgents wound up dying (36) than members of the security forces (11). Life in the capital has already returned to normal. When I was there a few weeks ago, I saw a thriving city where the biggest daily concerns are traffic jams and air pollution—not insurgent attacks.

The Allies Keep the Taliban Weak

The failure of this insurgent assault bodes well for Afghanistan's future—and runs counter to the doom-and-gloom in the U.S. The Taliban, Haqqanis and associated insurgents continue to enjoy safe havens in Pakistan, but the only way they will shoot their way back into power is if we abandon the vast majority of Afghans who have no desire to be ruled by ignorant, medieval tyrants.

Significant progress has been made in recent weeks in negotiating a long-term U.S.-Afghan security accord that the [Barack] Obama administration hopes to unveil at the NATO summit in Chicago next month [May 2012]. The two most contentious issues—"night raids" and the detention of Taliban prisoners by the U.S. military—were resolved by giving Afghan authorities more control while allowing essential operations to continue.

---

1. The Tet Offensive was a military attack by the North Vietnamese and Vietcong against the United States and its allies in the Vietnam War. A turning point in the war, the attack showed the strength of the Communist Vietnamese and took the Americans by surprise.

The bad news—and the reason so many well-to-do Afghans are talking of selling homes and businesses and moving abroad—is that there remain major concerns about how much support the U.S. will provide for Afghanistan when 70% of the American public has turned against the war.

Backing Off Will Strengthen the Taliban

The White House can take three specific steps to make clear the depth of our commitment. First, pledge to maintain a force of at least 68,000 troops through the end of 2014. Second, maintain a residual presence after 2014 of at least 30,000 troops to advise and assist Afghan forces. Third, maintain funding of at least $6 billion a year for the Afghan National Security Forces indefinitely.

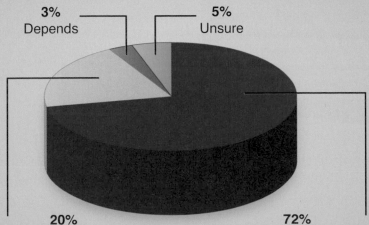

Troops Are Needed to Keep the Taliban in Check

A poll taken shortly after the death of Osama bin Laden in 2011 found that a large majority of Americans believed that even though the al Qaeda leader had been removed as a threat, the Taliban remained very dangerous, and thus US troops should remain in Afghanistan.

3%
Depends

5%
Unsure

20%
Remove US troops because the Taliban and al Qaeda are less of a threat with Bin Laden dead.

72%
Keep US troops in Afghanistan because the Taliban and al Qaeda are still a threat.

Taken from: NBC News Poll, May 5–7, 2011.

Unfortunately, there is serious reason to wonder if these conditions will be met. The president is already in the process of cutting the U.S. force—which peaked at 100,000 last year—by 32,000 troops. That drawdown will be completed by the end of September [2012], earlier than military commanders deem advisable. The withdrawal of these "surge" forces has imperiled plans to switch the counterinsurgency focus from southern to eastern Afghanistan where Haqqani sanctuaries remain intact a few hours' drive from Kabul.

If Troops Leave, Terrorists Return

I recently visited Khost Province on the border with Pakistan. Although this is a longtime Haqqani stronghold, both Khost and neighboring Paktia are garrisoned by only one U.S. brigade, or roughly 4,000 troops. The widespread fear is that once the U.S. troops leave, the Haqqanis will return. It is imperative that more U.S. troops be committed to clear such areas, but that may no longer be possible given the U.S. drawdown. So far plans call for only one additional brigade to be sent to the east—a unit from the 82nd Airborne Division that is moving into Logar Province south of Kabul.

Fast Fact

The International Security Assistance Force (ISAF) reports that as of mid-2012 there were about ninety thousand US troops in Afghanistan.

Even after 2014, barring a miraculous peace agreement with the Taliban, Afghanistan will need a robust American presence. Afghan troops are eager and skilled fighters—they rush into battle in unarmored pick-up trucks along bomb-strewn roads—but they need assistance with logistics, medevac flights, air support, intelligence collection, and other higher-level functions.

Providing that support will require a substantial contingent of American personnel who in turn will need more troops to protect and supply them. If U.S. force levels post-2014 are minuscule—say, the 5,000 troops that President Obama offered to leave in Iraq—they will not be able to protect themselves, much less carry out their mission.

US troops conduct a mission in Afghanistan's Khost Province. It is feared that once US troops leave the province the Haqqani and other militants will return.

We Can Win if We Stay

The bulk of future fighting must be carried out by the Afghans themselves, but in order to have any chance of success they must have enough troops to garrison a far-flung country of 30 million people. And that in turn will require outside funding. The Kabul government remains too impoverished to pay its own security costs.

Maintaining an Afghan force of 350,000 soldiers and police, the level which will be reached this year, will require $6 billion a year. Yet the Obama administration wants to provide only $4.1 billion a year. That would require laying off 120,000 soldiers and cops—a move that would significantly destabilize Afghanistan without producing significant savings in a $3.8 trillion U.S. budget.

If we avoid such unforced errors and stick with the plans developed by Gens. Stanley McChrystal, David Petraeus and John Allen, we have a good chance to maintain a pro-Western regime in power. The Taliban are too weak to defeat us or our Afghan allies. But we can defeat ourselves.

EVALUATING THE AUTHOR'S ARGUMENTS:

Both Max Boot and Rory Stewart, the author of the following viewpoint, have visited Afghanistan. Yet each paints very different pictures of the Afghan people's daily life, the level of violence with which they contend, and their attitudes toward Americans. In a few sentences, describe each author's take on life in Afghanistan. Then, state which author you think paints a more credible picture, and why.

US Troop Presence in Afghanistan Helped the Taliban Grow Strong

"The increases in foreign troops didn't improve security: rather the reverse."

Rory Stewart

In the following viewpoint Rory Stewart argues that increased troop presence in Afghanistan has bolstered the Taliban. He explains that right after the Taliban was toppled from power, the United States and its allies maintained a very light troop presence, and Afghanistan flourished. Schools, health clinics, and markets opened, utility services were expanded, and the country seemed headed in a productive direction. It was not until greater numbers of troops were sent to Afghanistan that violence increased. Stewart suggests that Afghans deeply resent the troops that foreigners have poured into their country. The Taliban have capitalized on this, he says, and have convinced Afghans to fight with them to overthrow the foreign occupation. Stewart says the foreign money given to political candidates, too, has made them seem illegitimate to their people. For all of these reasons he concludes that the US troop presence has strengthened the Taliban, and thus troops should be withdrawn.

Stewart is a member of the British Parliament and the author of *The Places in Between*, a memoir of his trip to north-central Afghanistan in 2002.

AS YOU READ, CONSIDER THE FOLLOWING QUESTIONS:
1. Why does Stewart think the Taliban are unlikely to again give terrorists shelter, as they did with al Qaeda leader Osama bin Laden in 2001?
2. What countries are more important to global and regional security than Afghanistan, according to the author?
3. How has Helmand Province changed between 2005 and 2011, according to Stewart?

The initial decision to strike back after the 9/11 attacks is easy to understand. History, however, will ask not why the West invaded Afghanistan, but why did it stay so long?

Why, a decade after 9/11, were there still 140,000 coalition troops on the ground? Why were there so many civilian casualties in May and June 2011—more than in any preceding recorded month? Why had the United States been in Afghanistan for twice the length of World War II?

The conventional answer to all these questions is that Afghanistan still poses an existential threat to global security. In March 2009, presenting his strategy for a surge in troop numbers, President [Barack] Obama said, "If the Afghan government falls to the Taliban . . . that country will again be a base for terrorists who want to kill as many of our people as they possibly can."

These fears are reinforced by a domino theory that if Afghanistan falls, Pakistan will follow, and the Taliban will get their hands on nuclear weapons.

Every one of these claims is wrong.

The Truth About the Taliban

First, Afghanistan poses less of a threat to global security than has been imagined. The Taliban are extremely unlikely to be able to seize Kabul, even if there was a very significant reduction in foreign troops. In the unlikely event they succeeded, they are even more unlikely to invite Al Qaeda back: Many Taliban leaders see that connection as their fundamental mistake before 9/11 and believe that if they had not supported Al Qaeda, they would still be in power.

And even with a foothold in Afghanistan, Al Qaeda wouldn't significantly strengthen its ability to harm the West. The U.S. would respond much more vigorously than it did before 9/11 if Al Qaeda bases were detected in Afghanistan, and the Taliban could offer little protection.

The Conventional Wisdom Is Wrong

If the question is about regional stability, Egypt is more important than Afghanistan. If the concern is terrorism, Pakistan is more important. And Pakistan's security won't be determined by events across the border but by its own internal politics, economic decline and toxic relationship with India. Afghanistan isn't strategically important enough to justify the West's current level of military and humanitarian investment—and failure there is inevitable unless we reverse course.

Consider the conventional wisdom that following the fall of Kabul, the West was distracted by Iraq and maintained too light a footprint in Afghanistan, failing to provide sufficient money or troops for the mission. Afghans who initially welcomed a foreign military intervention were alienated by the slow pace of development and the poor governance. This lack of progress created the opening for the Taliban to return. According to this narrative, it was only Obama's surge of 2009 that, in his words, "for the first time in years . . . put in place the strategy and resources" so that by December 2010, the U.S. was "on track to achieve (its) goals."

More Troops Hurt Afghanistan's Success

An irony is that the "light footprint" of the early years was relatively successful—Al Qaeda members were driven out of the country almost immediately, and very quickly, school attendance improved dramatically, health clinics were rolled out, and mobile telephone usage exploded. Non-state-controlled media outlets were established and elections were held for the first time in decades. These are accomplishments worthy of pride, but sadly, the addition of more troops and resources to the NATO [North Atlantic Treaty Organization]–led mission since 2006 has made the situation worse.

The tens of billions of dollars donated to the government of Afghanistan have undermined its leadership. The fashionable agendas of foreigners on short-term tours and their micromanagement have pushed aside the priorities of Afghan ministers. Many of the reconstruction projects have fueled waste and corruption. What's more, the increases in foreign troops didn't improve security: rather the reverse. Helmand is less safe in 2011 with 32,000 foreign troops in the province than it was in 2005, when there were only 300.

Violence and Resentment

When I walked alone across central Afghanistan in the winter of 2001 and 2002, I found Afghan villagers to be hospitable and generous, but also far more conservative, insular and Islamist than foreigners acknowledged. When I returned to the country in 2006, to establish a nonprofit organization, it was clear that their resistance was inflamed by the increasingly heavy presence of Western troops, which allowed the Taliban to gain support by presenting themselves as fighters for Islam and Afghanistan against a foreign occupation.

In June [2011], Obama announced a drawdown of U.S. forces, to be completed in 2014 with the handover of responsibility to Afghan forces. But a political settlement in the next three years is highly improbable because neither the Taliban, nor the Afghan government, nor Afghanistan's neighbors are showing much commitment to compromise, in part because they still believe they can win.

Author and British member of Parliament Rory Stewart (pictured) claims that the presence of NATO troops in Afghanistan has fostered resentment and violence among the Afghan population.

Western Involvement Has Undermined Progress

Many people have pointed out the absurdity of the West's approach. From 2008 to 2010, I ran the Carr Center for Human Rights Policy at Harvard's Kennedy School [of Government]. The center's research fellows collectively had more than a century of experience on the ground in Afghanistan. Research by fellows such as Andrew Wilder, David Mansfield and Michael Semple proved that our aid projects were increasing instability; that we were undermining any chance of political settlement with the Taliban; and that the Taliban-controlled areas were often more secure than the government areas. Their findings explained why our counterinsurgency strategy was empty and the "surge" was counterproductive, but they were often ignored by the military and political establishment, which has remained defiantly optimistic.

When the Taliban Win

US presence and other actions may give a boost to the Taliban, warns the International Council on Security and Development. The following table calculates what happens for the Afghan people—and the Taliban's standing—when the United States and its allies destroy poppy crops, bomb targets, and take other actions.

Factor	International Community Loss	Taliban Gain
Aggressive counter-narcotics policies	Having lost their livelihoods, people associate low quality of life with the international community.	Taliban finds favor in communities affected by eradication efforts. Where narcotics policies are failing to reduce cultivation in the long run, the Taliban is financing its operations from profits.
Aid donations not reaching intended recipients	Afghan people, suffering without necessary aid, will think it is only firepower that international forces are willing to contribute in the current chapter of their unending conflict.	Taliban has been known to capitalize on this, quickly filling ungoverned space and becoming the legitimate authority in the eyes of those let down by external forces.
Counterterrorism operation, rather than counter-insurgency	Current militant numbers may be reduced, but the core problems prompting a constant supply still remain, paving the way for future instability in Afghanistan.	Focus is on pinning down suspected militants rather than broader development, and so hopeless living conditions remain, in which it is easy for the insurgency to recruit disillusioned people.
Aerial bombings	Inability to control civilian casualties destroys any trust available from local people.	Taliban does not have the capability to carry out this kind of operation, and use the collateral damage accumulated by NATO as a selling point.
Military tactics	The scales will remain unbalanced while traditional warfare is being used against an irregular force. State-of-the-art equipment, including air support, has not proven a decisive tactical advantage.	Continued use of asymmetric tactics (some imported from insurgents in Iraq) continues to elude Western forces. Taliban possess advantages such as knowing the local terrain, being able to blend into local communities, and having the freedom to cross the border at southern and eastern points, where international troops are not mandated to pursue them.
Safe havens in Pakistan	Although Pakistan has recently stated a greater willingness/ability to exert pressure, years of inertia means that insurgents can be trained in relative safety just across the Afghan-Pakistan border.	This is both a diplomatic and practical bonus. With a force as strong as the United States reluctant to penetrate their bases, they are logistically invincible.

Over the last decade of war, many politicians have trusted charismatic, optimistic generals rather than their own instincts and reason. Concerns about the huge costs of the mission ($120 billion per year for the U.S. alone) and exaggerated fears about what would follow if it failed co-opted almost everyone: Afghan businessmen and foreign contractors, writers and academics. All continued to hope that some magic plan would extract us from humiliation.

At the heart of our irrational persistence are the demons of guilt and fear. Leaders are hypnotized by fears about global security; feel guilty about the loss of lives; ashamed at their inability to honor our promises to Afghans; and terrified of admitting defeat.

Failure in Afghanistan has become "not an option." This is the fatal legacy of 9/11, because with that slogan, failure has become invisible, inconceivable and inevitable.

EVALUATING THE AUTHOR'S ARGUMENTS:

In the previous viewpoint Max Boot says the United States should give more money to Afghan leaders to help them maintain the high costs of security. In this viewpoint, however, Rory Stewart suggests that giving money to Afghan leaders has made them look like foreign powers' puppets and is among the actions that have strengthened the Taliban. After reading both viewpoints, with which author do you agree? Explain your reasoning.

The Taliban Seek Nuclear Weapons

Jay J. Schlickman

> *"The possibility of a terrorist confiscation of Pakistan's nuclear warheads would radically degrade American security and with it the safety of all Western society."*

Jay J. Schlickman is an industrial physicist and a veteran of the Korean War. In the following viewpoint he warns that the Taliban could buy or steal nuclear weapons, which would have nightmarish results. Afghanistan is next to Pakistan, which owns many powerful nuclear weapons and long-range missiles. It is unclear how safe these weapons are in Pakistan. Although the Pakistani government and other sources say the weapons are safe and well guarded, Pakistani nuclear scientists have in the past leaked information to terrorist or other unfriendly groups. Schlickman imagines it would not be too difficult for the Taliban to get these weapons and warns they would not hesitate to use them to kill tens of millions of people or sell them to other rogue groups who would do the same. He urges American leaders to take seriously the possibility that the Taliban could get their hands on nuclear weapons.

AS YOU READ, CONSIDER THE FOLLOWING QUESTIONS:
1. How many nuclear weapons does the author say are owned by Pakistan?
2. Why should the Pakistani government not be trusted to adequately safeguard their weapons, according to Schlickman?
3. Who is Abdul Qadeer Khan, as cited by the author?

O n Sept. 22 [2011] in Orlando the GOP [Republican] presidential candidates were given the hypothetical scenario of a 3 a.m. call to the president that the Taliban had captured the Pakistan government's nuclear-weapons cache. The candidates' response to the scenario was at best disconcerting and at worst woefully naïve.

To understand the implications of this nightmare it is best to begin with an examination of what such an act of terror could lead to.

The Taliban Could Steal and Sell Nukes

First, based on a lengthy and extraordinarily detailed Wikipedia report, the Pakistani nuclear-weapon cache consists of at least 100 nuclear-tipped weapons capable of at least Hiroshima-level detonations [i.e., about fifteen thousand tons of TNT explosives].

Many fear that the Taliban may steal nuclear weapons from Pakistan's arsenal and sell them to Iran or North Korea.

Second, it would be relatively easy for the Taliban to sell the atomic bombs to countries such as Iran and North Korea that have advanced delivery capabilities.

Third, although the Pakistani cache is supposed to be widely dispersed to increase security, the bombs are located in a relatively lawless country. [Former al Qaeda leader] Osama bin Laden reposed there for years within an arms length of the central government, and Admiral Michael Mullen [former chairman of the Joint Chiefs of Staff] has alerted us to the probable duplicity of the Pakistani government in the murders of our troops.

Most importantly, their chief atomic scientist, Abdul Qadeer Khan, had no compunction about smuggling both the design and critical physical technology of nuclear warheads throughout the terrorist world.

Obviously, the possibility of a terrorist confiscation of Pakistan's nuclear warheads would radically degrade American security and with it the safety of all Western society.

Millions Could Be Killed

Contrast our economic concerns against the nightmare of a nuclear conflagration. For example, the level of economic pain would be relatively imperceptible compared to the pain that would be felt by millions of human beings as the result of a nuclear fireball. The level of economic pain would be background noise compared to the horror of a global holocaust where the number of people placed in concentration camps would make the 60 million killed in the world wars of the 20th century look like a dress rehearsal for the 21st century.

Taking This Threat Seriously

The critical importance of our economy is no reason for our presidential candidates to be so unaware of their role in the sanctity of our country.

Could the Taliban Get Nuclear Weapons?

Security experts think there is a legitimate risk militants could seize weapons or bomb-making material from nearby Pakistan.

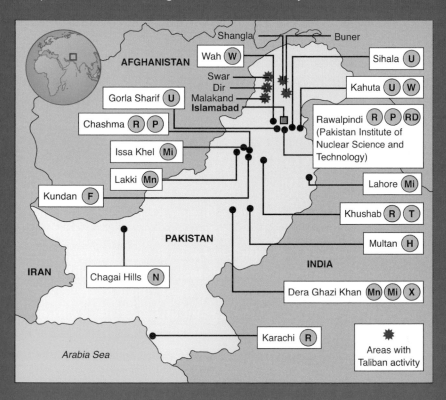

F Fuel Fabrication

H Heavy Water

Mi Milling

Mn Mining

N Nuclear Testing

P Plutonium Reprocessing

R Reactors

RD Research and Development

T Tritium Production

U Uranium (U) Enrichment

X U-Hexaflouride Conversion

W Weaponization

What they should have said without hesitation and reservation is that the White House would, under such a circumstance, immediately call for intensive and extensive military strikes to remove the threat with no limit placed upon the offensive scope and intensity. This is the type of message that we yearn for from our leaders. This is the clear, unequivocal warning to all Islamists that we have had a belly full of their vile barbarism and that we are sick and tired of American covert appeasement that has become the hallmark of U.S. politics.

The GOP candidates may have been the first on the firing line and failed, but we still need to know the answer from the current administration.

EVALUATING THE AUTHOR'S ARGUMENTS:

Jay J. Schlickman and Feroz Hassan Khan (author of the following viewpoint) hold different opinions on whether the West should fear a nuclear Taliban. After reading both viewpoints, what is your opinion? How vulnerable are Pakistani nuclear weapons? Are the Taliban likely to get them? Explain your reasoning and include evidence from the text that swayed you.

The Taliban Are Unlikely to Obtain Nuclear Weapons

Feroz Hassan Khan

"The fear that Pakistani nuclear weapons could fall into the hands of the Taliban is totally misplaced."

In the following viewpoint Feroz Hassan Khan argues that the Taliban are unlikely to obtain nuclear weapons from Pakistan. He says it is completely irrational to think that Pakistani forces might help the Taliban get such weapons. Although it is more possible that the Taliban might steal or sabotage nuclear weapons, Khan details the numerous ways in which the Pakistani nuclear arsenal has been safeguarded in the years since the September 11 terrorist attacks. Khan says most fears about the Taliban obtaining nuclear weapons are based on hype, fear, or gross exaggeration—the reality, in his opinion, is that Pakistani nuclear weapons are well guarded and unlikely to fall into the hands of the Taliban or anyone else.

Khan is the former director of arms control and disarmament affairs in the Strategic Plans Division of the Joint Services Headquarters of Pakistan.

Feroz Hassan Khan, "Nuclear Security in Pakistan: Separating Myth from Reality," Arms Control Association, July 8, 2009.

AS YOU READ, CONSIDER THE FOLLOWING QUESTIONS:
1. What, according to Khan, is a "bizarre" fear to have about Pakistani nuclear weapons?
2. How many troops are in Pakistan's armed forces, according to Khan?
3. Describe Pakistan's system of sensitive material control and accounting, as described by the author.

Pakistan is passing through an extremely delicate phase in its history. Recent instability in Pakistan, including the Taliban's advance into settled areas, prompted the Pakistani military to undertake large-scale military operations in the Swat Valley. As military and Taliban forces fight in the rugged tribal terrain, several Western analysts have raised concerns about the future of nuclear Pakistan.

Fears About Pakistan's Nukes

The nightmare specter of nuclear weapons, nuclear material, or a whole country falling into al Qaeda or Taliban hands is invoked, creating fear and mistrust between critical allies in the war against terrorism. The risk of a dangerous policy outcome in the United States, based on flawed assumptions, is now far greater than the probability either of nuclear weapons falling into the hands of Taliban and other extremists or of the disintegration of Pakistan itself. Any misstep against a nervous nuclear-armed country would be a greater mistake than any made in Iraq. Fortunately, the current top leadership in the United States [the Barack Obama administration] can distinguish reality from myth. Nevertheless, misperceptions about weapons of mass destruction have influenced U.S. decisions too recently to be ignored in a discussion of the current situation in Pakistan.

Western fears about Pakistani nuclear security range from valid to bizarre. The more valid concerns involve theft of material, sabotage, unauthorized use of nuclear weapons, and insider-outsider collaboration. The potential for terrorist infiltration into the program is a concern for Western analysts and the Pakistani nuclear establishment. The bizarre fear involves the allegation that Pakistani armed forces and intelligence agencies, who are the custodians and guardians of the nuclear arsenal, could be accomplices to such an act as Taliban sympathizers. An alternate scenario posits that the inability of the armed forces to defeat the Taliban extremists would result in abdication of the Pakistani state to the Taliban. Gen. Tariq Majid, chairman of Pakistan's Joint Chiefs of Staff Committee, called such scenarios "plain mischievous" and said they "need to be contemptuously dismissed."

America Must Proceed Rationally

President Franklin D. Roosevelt famously said, "The only thing we have to fear is fear itself." His words aptly describe the prevalent fears in regard to the situation in Pakistan today. Two main dangers emanate from the hype on nuclear insecurity in Pakistan. The first danger is that the grossly exaggerated threat perception in the West may prompt the United States into policy choices it would later regret. The second danger is that continuing media focus on this issue stokes Pakistani paranoia about U.S. intentions. These fears and suspicions about U.S. intervention inside Pakistan could provoke that country to take defensive actions against foreign intervention rather than focusing on the possibility of reducing internal threats to nuclear security and could further fan anti-U.S. public sentiment. It is true that stability in Pakistan is shaky, its fledgling democracy is in transition, and it is facing internal threats from extremists. Until recently, decision-makers in Pakistan were in a state of denial and reacted only when the Taliban threat exploded in their faces. Therefore, it is justified to worry and ask questions about the security of a nuclear-armed country undergoing such a traumatic experience. It would be equally correct to weigh the seriousness of the threat against the ability of the state's security apparatus and its nuclear security measures to prevent the worst from happening. . . .

Fears Are "Totally Misplaced"

States managing a nuclear weapons program typically have three main types of nuclear security concerns. First, every nuclear-capable state worries about the external threat of a preventive strike by hostile powers against its nuclear facilities. Second, such states worry about physical invasion of the state by a hostile neighbor. The third and probably the most dangerous concern is insider-outsider collaboration. Pakistan has lived with all three categories of threats since the inception of its nuclear program. Like every state, Pakistan's program places great emphasis on secrecy and compartmentalization. In the past, no single office, organization, or authority held ultimate responsibility for supervision. For the past decade, there has been a National Command Authority (NCA) with a dedicated secretariat (the Strategic Plans Division, or SPD), which is responsible for all nuclear-related activities. Since these institutions were established, events, controversies, and deterioration of the regional and domestic environment have forced Pakistan to tighten its oversight and control.

The Taliban threat within Pakistan is a new phenomenon. The militant group led by Baitullah Mehsud belonging to the tribal belt in Waziristan calls itself the Tehrik-e-Taliban (TTP). The TTP is an extremist fringe whose activities have now expanded from the tribal areas into the settled areas of Pakistan. This provoked military operations that continue today and have resulted in the displacement of millions of people. The exact size of the Taliban in Pakistan is not known, but estimates range from 5,000 to 15,000. Grisly practices such as the public flogging of a young woman in April [2009], against a backdrop of kidnapping, bombings of schools and mosques, and general killing of innocent civilians, turned the Pakistani public against any accommodation with the TTP or any other religious extremist organization. The tipping point arrived when the TTP exploited the "peace deal" and advanced further inland. The Pakistani public was shocked at the actions of an elected government that abdicated to such a force by negotiating a deal.

Pakistan's armed forces are a half-million strong, and the country has a moderate Muslim populace with a history of repeatedly rejecting religious political parties. The country has reacted forcefully against

FAST FACT

According to the Federation of American Scientists, about twenty thousand nuclear weapons exist between the nine countries that are believed to possess them.

the Taliban, so the fear that Pakistani nuclear weapons could fall into the hands of the Taliban is totally misplaced. As explained by Naeem Salik in a recent op-ed, there is "no causal relationship between the military operations against the Taliban and the security of Pakistan's nuclear arsenal." . . .

Security Has Greatly Improved

Nuclear security culture evolved in Pakistan after the September 11 [2001] attacks. Pakistan improved its supervisory procedure for military and scientific manpower. The security division of the SPD established a reporting system for monitoring the movements of all officials. Two identical programs for employment security were created: the Personnel Reliability Program (PRP) and the Human Reliability Program (HRP), for military and civilian personnel, respectively. A security clearance system of annual, semiannual, and quarterly review was created. Counter Intelligence Teams were created to act as the daily eyes and ears of the SPD. Weekly, monthly, and quarterly reports for the security of all organizations are maintained by the SPD to prevent theft, loss, or accident.

Next, a system of sensitive material control and accounting was introduced. The system was derived from modern training, possibly modeled on U.S. national laboratory procedures. The system involved regular and surprise inspections to tally material production and waste in order to maintain transparency and accountability. Under a careful, secret plan instituted by the SPD, professional guards at static sites and escorts with tight security procedures are involved during transportation. Special theft- and tamper-proof vehicles and containers are used. In peacetime, nuclear weapons are not mated with their delivery systems and are not operationally deployed. Operational secrecy precludes specific discussion of management of nuclear arsenals, but a two-man rule and, in some cases, a three-man rule is followed, with physical safety and firewalls built into the weapon system to prevent any unauthorized launch.

Inspections, Training, and Oversight

The inception of the Nuclear Security Action Plan (NSAP), organized by the Pakistan Nuclear Regulatory Authority (PNRA), was a very important development in Pakistan's nuclear security management.

Chairman of Pakistan's Joint Chiefs of Staff, General Tariq Majid (right), says fears that terrorists will steal nuclear weapons from Pakistan's arsenal are totally misplaced.

The PNRA is an independent body responsible for civilian programs, but it coordinates closely with the SPD. The two organizations complement each other by sharing best practices.

The main task of the NSAP is to manage all nuclear activities and radioactive sources that are under regulatory control and to develop a sustainable national system. Nuclear security emergency centers and procedures to secure orphan radioactive sources and to secure borders against any illicit trafficking have been put in place. Rigorous inspections are one key element of the PNRA's activities to strengthen controls. Another is the training of a wide variety of personnel from all major organizations. The training involves nuclear security, physical protection, emergency preparedness, detection equipment, recovery operations, and border monitoring. The organizations involved in training are the Coast Guard, Frontier Corps, Pakistan Rangers, Customs, Emergency & Rescue Services, National Disaster Management Cell, intelligence services, law enforcement agencies, and all strategic organizations including offices from the SPD.

A Nuclear Security Emergency Coordination Center has been established in Islamabad [Pakistan's largest city], which is the focal point of coordination, by all the government agencies mentioned above. In addition, regional offices in all major cities have been established, creating a network of six emergency-response mobile laboratories. The primary job of this network, which was completed in December 2008, is to track and respond to any threat of illicit nuclear material, a radioactive source, or a radiological dispersion device ("dirty bomb"). Finally, the NSAP has established border controls at major crossing points with state-of-the-art screening procedures with the help of the IAEA [International Atomic Energy Agency] and the U.S. Department of Energy. . . .

Pakistan's Nukes Are Safe

Despite widely known limitations, Pakistan has done remarkably well in establishing a nuclear security regime and an evolving nuclear security culture that requires encouragement and support. It has been quite liberal in briefing U.S. officials, academics, and even journalists about its nuclear management. Over several years, Pakistan has sent officials, technicians, and administrators to receive training on modern technical solutions and management under the aegis of mutually acceptable arrangements that cater to each side's sensitivities.

EVALUATING THE AUTHOR'S ARGUMENTS:

In this viewpoint Feroz Hassan Khan downplays fears that the Taliban might obtain nuclear weapons from Pakistan. What pieces of evidence does he provide to support this claim? Does he convince you of his argument? Explain why or why not.

Chapter 2

What Is the Relationship Between the Taliban and Afghanistan's Drug Trade?

A farmer tends his poppy crop in Afghanistan. Just how much the drug trade impacts the war in Afghanistan is of much debate.

The Taliban Are Strengthened by Afghanistan's Opium Trade

"In areas where the Taliban are dominant, the village-level Taliban subcommander will hand out written receipts for the amount of opium collected."

Gretchen Peters

The Taliban are bankrolled by Afghanistan's booming drug trade, argues Gretchen Peters in the following viewpoint. She details several ways in which the Taliban profit from the country's opium trade. They levy taxes on farmers who grow opium and also make money by charging local drug lords to protect their warehouses and trade routes. Proceeds from these activities pay for fuel, transport vehicles, weaponry, explosive supplies, food, insurgent salaries, and more. Peters concludes that Afghanistan's lucrative opium trade directly benefits the Taliban and makes it possible for them to continue the fight against US and allied forces.

Peters is a journalist who has covered Pakistan and Afghanistan for more than a decade. Her articles have been published by the Associated Press and ABC News. She is the author of *Seeds of Terror: How Heroin Is Bankrolling the Taliban and al Qaeda* (2009).

AS YOU READ, CONSIDER THE FOLLOWING QUESTIONS:
1. How many hectares of poppies were harvested in Afghanistan in 2000 and in 2002, according to Peters?
2. What, according to Peters, do Taliban commanders use like an ATM machine?
3. What is paramilitary Force 333, according to the author?

The 2001 invasion of Afghanistan caused the Taliban and al-Qaeda to scatter but failed to put down either group once and for all. Rather than mounting a nationwide invasion with vast numbers of foreign troops, the United States and its allies opted for a "light-footprint" approach, relying on local proxies. Many senior al-Qaeda and Taliban leaders fled over the border into Pakistan. Numerous mid-level Taliban lay low in Afghanistan's Pashto southwest, often in the fertile plains of western Kandahar and Helmand that also cultivated poppy. "There was no coordinated effort—they just escaped to places where they knew they'd find safe haven," said journalist Rahimullah Yusufzai. . . .

Increased Poppy Cultivation

In the spring following the invasion, poppy fields carpeted the Afghan countryside. The year before the invasion, Afghan farmers had harvested just 8,000 hectares—mostly in areas outside the Taliban's control, according to the UNODC [United Nations Office on Drugs and Crime]. In 2002, the total land area planted with poppy surged to 74,000 hectares, returning Afghanistan to its spot as the world's leading opium producer. Across the border, agents from Pakistan's Anti-Narcotics Force ambushed a camel convoy in the Baloch desert. The camels lugged nearly a ton of heroin and morphine base on their backs. Worth tens of millions of dollars, it was, at the time, one of the biggest drug hauls the world had ever seen.

With few foreign troops posted outside Kandahar city, a dangerous security vacuum developed in the Pashto south. The Taliban quietly began to regroup, and commanders started reaching out to one another. Mullah Omar reportedly contacted his deputies one by one and appointed them to organize his fighters, pick up fresh recruits from Pakistani madrassas [Muslim schools], locate weapons stashes, and raise funds. Drug smugglers close to the Taliban were some of the first investors, putting up small amounts of funds to help the movement start to rebuild, according to sources close to the Taliban interviewed for this study. Many commanders raised money by selling off opium stores they had hidden away, these sources said. . . .

Since 2001, Taliban commanders have diversified their activities within the opium trade. Examining the various ways Taliban commanders and members of the top leadership earn profit from narcotics illustrates how the myriad drug earnings enter the system.

Taxing Opium

Taliban insurgents tax farmers in their control zones. Researchers for this study were told that Taliban commanders collect the full 10-percent *ushr* [tax/tithe] in some districts, while in others, commanders and local Mullahs share the take, according to a 2008 British report. In areas where the Taliban are dominant, the village-level Taliban sub-commander will hand out written receipts for the amount of opium collected, and farmers interviewed for this study said the Taliban leadership was strict in assigning each commander's control zone. Researchers for this study heard multiple cases in which farmers complained to the Taliban leadership of being overcharged, and the Quetta Shura

The author says that profits from the Afghan drug trade enable the Taliban to buy weapons to continue their struggle against US and allied forces.

responded by punishing the subcommanders. Likewise, Taliban commanders keep track of how much farmers and other members of the local community are earning by maintaining informants in each community, paying the equivalent of $10 a tip for information. In areas where there was no clear dominant force, there are reports of fighting between Taliban commanders, criminal gangs, and corrupt officials, who all appear to prey on the farmers. . . .

The Taliban's Opium Warehouses

In the rural environment, where there is little use for hard cash, much economic dealing is done in opium and other commodities of value. The Taliban maintain opium warehouses across Afghanistan's southern poppy heartland, where insurgent commanders can deposit and later withdraw quantities of opium as if using an ATM machine. In December 2007, NATO [North Atlantic Treaty Organization] forces that retook Musa Qala [a district in northern Helmand Province] found 11 tons of opium stored in warehouses there. Taliban commanders at the village level also appear to receive millions of dollars each year worth of material supplies collected as tax from villagers and smugglers, although it is impossible to calculate an accurate total value for such barter deals. They often include vehicles, such as motorcycles, SUVs, or pickup trucks. Many commanders demand satellite and mobile telephones, or will collect top-up [prepaid phone] cards with talk-time credit from local shopkeepers. Other supplies they take as payment include weapons, ammunition, petrol [gasoline], food, shelter, and even medical care for wounded soldiers.

Opium Money Keeps the Taliban Operational

Proceeds from *ushr,* as well as commodities collected in barter deals, appear to supply village and district-level Taliban with the bulk of their operational needs, everything from salaries for fighters and transport, fuel, food, weapons, and explosives. Each village-level subcommander must pay a percentage of the proceeds he collects to his military commander at the district level, who in turns pays off the district-level Taliban governor. A portion of these funds—still often transferred in the form of raw or partially refined opium—then reportedly filter up the Taliban chain of command to the provincial commander, who will hand over a portion to the Taliban's central financial committee. Because of the lower degree of command and control among the insurgents relative to their time in power during the 1990s, it would appear that the percentages of money sent up the chain of command vary across the southern conflict zone. And although researchers for this study heard multiple cases of Taliban commanders battling over drug spoils, in general, commanders all appeared to pay into the system, much as local mafiosi [mobsters] might hand a portion of their earnings to their boss.

Protection Money

Providing protection for the opium trade is another lucrative form of earning for the Taliban in the south. It is common in Afghanistan for a local power broker—be they Taliban or not—to take a cut of commodities moving through his patch, or to receive payments for providing armed protection for a shipment as it passes. More than 65 percent of people surveyed for this study said the Taliban's main activities related to drugs were providing security for opium crops as they grew and then protecting drug shipments as they leave the farm area. These fees can range up to 20 percent of the consignment, according to dozens of interviews with truckers and officials. Almost half those surveyed for this study described how low-level al-Qaeda operatives and other foreign *jihadi*

FAST FACT

The United Nations reports that 90 percent of the world's heroin comes from Afghanistan.

[Muslim religious warriors] groups, such as the Islamic Movement of Uzbekistan (IMU), provide security for shipments as they move out of Afghanistan—precisely the stage where one stands to profit most.

An Expanded Protection Racket

Insurgents have broadly expanded their activities in the protection racket since 2001. In return for taxes they collect, the Taliban provide security for poppy farmers, building defensive positions around their fields or planting mines and IEDs [improvised explosive devices] ahead of visits by the eradication police. According to Afghan and NATO officials, Taliban units have also attacked security checkpoints to allow drug convoys to pass, and on occasion have even launched diversionary strikes to draw Western troops away from an area where a major consignment was passing. They have come to the protection of drug

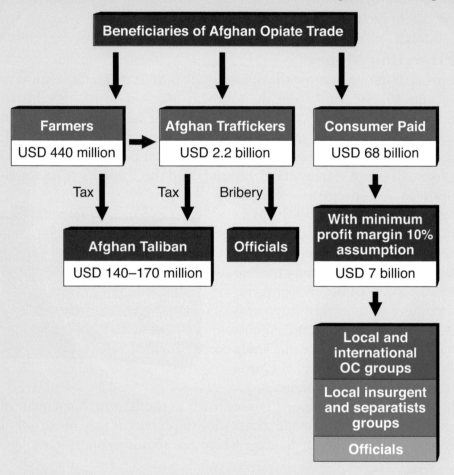

Who Benefits from Opiate Trafficking?

The United Nations Office on Drugs and Crime estimates the Taliban take away between $140 million and $170 million from Afghanistan's drug trade.

Beneficiaries of Afghan Opiate Trade

Farmers
USD 440 million

Afghan Traffickers
USD 2.2 billion

Consumer Paid
USD 68 billion

Tax   Tax   Bribery

Afghan Taliban
USD 140–170 million

Officials

With minimum profit margin 10% assumption
USD 7 billion

Local and international OC groups

Local insurgent and separatists groups

Officials

Taken from: *The Global Afghan Opium Trade: A Threat Assessment.* United Nations Office on Drugs and Crime, July 2011.

labs being raided by the paramilitary Force 333, according to a former commander of Force 333. "One time we went to raid a big lab in the Deshu district of Baram Cha," a major center for heroin production in southern Helmand, he said. "Within twenty minutes there was a massive ambush. Bullets were flying everywhere." The lab owner had called the local Taliban subcommander to come to his rescue. The attack was so vicious the Force 333 commander had to call in air support from the American military to suppress the attack.

Campaigns for territorial gain, such as a 2007 Taliban push into Deh Rawood district in Uruzgan, have been launched to aid smuggling activities. Deh Rawood is perched along the most important drugs- and arms-trafficking route in Uruzgan, connecting to Iran in the west and Pakistan in the south. The shift in battlefield tactics is a strong indication Taliban leaders work closely with traffickers, who appear to have tremendous decision-making influence over their strategic activities. This transformation in their battlefield tactics—from trying to make tactical gains to protecting drug shipments—mirrors similar behavior by insurgent groups around the globe. Many Taliban are no longer fighting for Allah [God] but for the almighty dollar.

Heroin Labs

As they did during their time in power, Taliban insurgents collect taxes at drug refineries located near the Pakistan and Iran borders. Over time, some commanders took to running refineries themselves. When Afghan and international troops retook Musa Qala in December 2007, the Associated Press reported that the militants "oversaw heroin production" at as many as fifty heroin labs—and that the number of labs in operation expanded during their time in power. Some employed as many as sixty men. Meanwhile, the number of sites turning opium into crystal heroin, the high-end product exported to the West, climbed from thirty to fifty by 2008. More simple rigs making morphine base operated off the back of souped-up pickups that can hurtle across the rocky terrain hugging the Pakistan border.

EVALUATING THE AUTHOR'S ARGUMENTS:

Gretchen Peters and the authors of the following viewpoint agree that money from Afghanistan's drug trade benefits the Taliban, but they disagree on the extent to which this is a problem and on what the United States should do about it. After reading both viewpoints, which did you find more persuasive? Why?

Viewpoint 2

The Taliban's Benefit from the Drug Trade Has Been Exaggerated

Jonathan P. Caulkins,
Jonathan D. Kulick, and
Mark A.R. Kleiman

"To the extent that counternarcotics efforts succeed, they are more likely to increase than to reduce the revenues and power of the Taliban."

In the following viewpoint Jonathan P. Caulkins, Jonathan D. Kulick, and Mark A.R. Kleiman claim to dispel myths about the Taliban and Afghanistan's drug trade. They acknowledge that the Taliban profit from the drug trade, but argue they do so ineffectively—the Taliban only capture a small percentage of opium profits, and the extent to which these monies bankroll their operations is exaggerated. More importantly, they warn, eradicating Afghan's drug industry might motivate the Taliban to switch to a new industry that would be even more profitable for them.

The authors also suggest that taking hard-line stances against Afghanistan's opium industry—such as destroying poppy growers' fields—could alienate Afghans and encourage them to join the Taliban, which would strengthen the group even more. The authors conclude that antidrug operations tend to help America's enemies rather than hurt them, and they advise policy makers to avoid cracking down on Afghanistan's opium industry more than necessary.

Caulkins is Stever Professor of Operations Research and Public Policy at Carnegie Mellon University; Kulick is senior project manager at the Pepperdine University School of Public Policy; and Kleiman is a professor of public policy at the University of California, Los Angeles.

AS YOU READ, CONSIDER THE FOLLOWING QUESTIONS:
1. About what percentage of the total drug trade profits do the Taliban take in, according to the authors?
2. Americans consume what percentage of the world's illegal opium, according to Caulkins, Kulick, and Kleiman?
3. What is the concept of "alternative development" as described by the authors?

"*The Afghan Drug Industry Mostly Benefits the Taliban.*" Far from it. Today, Afghanistan essentially holds a monopoly on heroin exports to the Old World. The country accounts for more than 90 percent of global production; although drug markets evolve over time, Afghanistan's production costs are so much lower than its would-be competitors' that it is a safe bet to assume the country will be the leader for at least five or 10 more years.

Myths About the Taliban and the Drug Trade
In the popular and American political imaginations, the Taliban are thought to be the big winners from this near monopoly, and there is some truth to this. The "narcoterrorist" label is often misused, but the Taliban are the real deal. They really do use profits from the opium trade to finance terrorist attacks on civilian and military targets. Although the Taliban traffic only modest quantities entirely on their own, taxing other people's drug deals is an important source of revenue; no one knows how much the Taliban profit from the drug trade, but whether they do isn't up for serious debate.

But just because the Taliban benefit from the heroin business doesn't mean the heroin business mostly benefits the Taliban. Consider the numbers (or at least the rough ones—production figures fluctuate from year to year, conversion rates are crude estimates, and price data beyond the opium bazaars are sketchy). In a typical year, Afghan farmers sell about 7,000 tons of opium at $130 a kilogram to traffickers who convert that into 1,000 tons of heroin, worth perhaps $2,500 a kilogram in Afghanistan and $4,000 at wholesale in neighboring countries. That works out to roughly $900 million in annual revenues for the farmers, $1.6 billion for traffickers from operations within Afghanistan, and another $1.5 billion for those who smuggle heroin out of the country. (2010 was atypical; a poppy blight drove opium production down and prices up.)

The Taliban's take is subject to debate, with responsible estimates varying from $70 million to $500 million—but either way it's not a big slice of the pie. The Taliban take 2 to 12 percent of a $4 billion industry; farmers, traffickers, smugglers, and corrupt officials collectively earn much more. It is not clear why the Taliban have been so unsuccessful at translating their power and influence into a larger share of trafficker revenues, but one thing is clear: They have nowhere to go but up. Upsetting the apple cart just to see where it lands is ill-advised; to the extent that counternarcotics efforts succeed, they are more likely to increase than to reduce the revenues and power of the Taliban.

Do U.S. Drug Addicts Support the Taliban?

"American Drug Addicts Are Supporting the Taliban."

Hardly. In the months following the 9/11 attacks, the Office of National Drug Control Policy ran public service announcements implying that American drug users were supporting terrorists targeting the United States. In fact, while users in the United States are supporting plenty of unsavory characters, they aren't likely to be in Afghanistan. The big money in U.S. drug markets is still in cocaine, all of which is produced in the Western Hemisphere.

The United States consumes only about 5 percent of the world's illegal opium, and most of that comes from Colombia and Mexico. Most Afghan opiates, meanwhile, never leave Asia—they are that continent's health problem, and to a lesser extent Europe's. Iran and

"At last, some good news about farming."

"Bumper Harvest in Afghanistan—At last, some good news about farming," cartoon by Grizelda, www.Cartoon Stock.com. Copyright © Grizelda. Reproduction rights obtainable from www.CartoonStock.com.

Russia may have a stake in Afghan exports, but protecting those countries' citizens from drug abuse is not obviously a major U.S. interest unless the Russian and Iranian governments are willing to offer something of value in exchange. . . .

Hard-Line Measures May Alienate Afghans
"Destroying Afghan Farmers' Poppy Fields Is a Bad Idea."
Often, but not always. In the early years of the Afghanistan war, coalition policy included widespread forced eradication [of poppy

fields]. In June 2009, however, Barack Obama's administration announced that U.S. and other international forces would no longer conduct eradication operations, on which the late [American diplomat] Richard Holbrooke said the United States had "wasted hundreds of millions of dollars."

The sensible motivation for this reversal was recognition that eradication produced unintended consequences. Pulling up a farmer's opium crop could generate ill will, perhaps enough to produce a new recruit for the insurgency. It was also geographically inconvenient. Afghanistan is a horrendously complicated place, but to oversimplify, two-thirds of the country (roughly 27 of 34 provinces) has been nearly poppy-free and relatively stable for a few years. The remaining third—in particular Helmand and Kandahar provinces—is rife with both poppies and insurgents. Eradication in those areas has a minimal and temporary effect on the drug trade, at most pushing production to the next valley or district. And angering farmers where Taliban recruiters prowl seemed like a gift to the enemy. So the Obama administration swore off direct support of eradication, though the governors of some Afghan provinces continue to pursue their own eradication programs.

But swearing off eradication everywhere has come with its own unintended consequences. Two-thirds of Afghanistan has—at considerable cost—been largely rid of poppies already. Keeping them poppy-free is not only relatively easy at this point, but will maintain a degree of normalcy for more than half the country, placate Russia—which, as one of the principal markets for Afghan drugs, is understandably irate at the prospect of a hands-off opium policy—and cement the United States' local reputation for being opposed to drugs at a time when addiction is sweeping Afghan society. If America wants to win hearts and minds in a country whose addiction rate is among the highest in the world, there are worse things than being seen as resolutely anti-drug while reminding people that the Taliban profit from the illicit industry that has enslaved their family members. Refraining from quixotic and counterproductive measures in the south does not require sacrificing progress already made in the rest of the country.

The Lesser of Two Evils

"Everyone Would Be Better Off If Afghan Farmers Grew Something Else."

Not necessarily. Alternative development—sometimes called "alternative livelihoods"—is the kinder, gentler complement to eradication. Both target farmers, the thinking goes, but one plants crops and bulldozes roads, while the other bulldozes crops and plants resentment. Even if alternative development doesn't meaningfully reduce worldwide drug cultivation—and it doesn't—at least the do-gooders do no harm, right?

Wrong. The Taliban tax opium not because the Quran [Muslim holy book] opposes intoxicants; they tax opium because it is taxable. In the lawless stretches of Afghanistan, the Taliban, local warlords, corrupt officials, and anyone else with enough guns all extort "protection" payments from almost any activity undertaken in their zone of control—including alternative-development projects. The *Wall Street Journal* reported last summer [2010] that half the electricity produced by a U.S. Agency for International Development–funded $100 million upgrade to a hydropower plant in Helmand province is effectively sold by the Taliban. Even if one dismisses such egregious examples, back-of-the-envelope calculations of the overall impact are not encouraging. Multiply the commonly acknowledged 10 to 20 percent extortion "tax" rate levied by the Taliban by the total international budget for alternative development in Afghanistan, and you get a revenue stream well in excess of what the Taliban is thought to derive from the opium trade.

No one doubts that development needs to be a major part of the agenda in Afghanistan, but there is a strong case to be made for using these programs as a reward for stabilized provinces—not a means of winning over hostile ones.

Less Is More

"The Afghan Drug Problem is Beyond Hope."

Not if we're patient. If solutions must be quick or decisive, then counternarcotics in Afghanistan is no solution. But that does not

An Afghan policeman supervises the destruction of a poppy field. Many critics say that destroying the poppy fields hurts Afghan farmers and civilians more than it does the Taliban.

mean that nothing can or should be done. Small steps are better than no steps, and even in a land in such desperate circumstances, giving up makes for bad public relations.

There are practical options. The United States could fund drug treatment in Afghanistan, a country with a horrendous heroin problem, to reduce demand and earn support from the Afghan public. It could encourage consumer countries (including Iran and Russia) to step up drug treatment; that will shrink the revenues of Afghan traffickers. Focusing alternative-development efforts on more stable parts of the country, as a reward for taking steps toward normalcy, could further erode the threat of the Taliban gaining influence there. And removing Afghan officials corrupted by the drug trade from seats of power—if it were possible—would bolster confidence in the government.

It would be foolish to expect too much from these approaches. But the limitations of feasible drug-control activities in Afghanistan do not justify continuing to pursue policies that do more harm than good. Because the natural tendency of counternarcotics efforts is to help America's enemies, the country should pursue them as little as possible. This is a case where less really is more.

EVALUATING THE AUTHOR'S ARGUMENTS:

To make their argument, Jonathan P. Caulkins, Jonathan D. Kulick, and Mark A.R. Kleiman posit a commonly held belief about Afghanistan's drug trade and then spend the following text discrediting it. What is your opinion of this narrative technique? Did you think it was an effective way for the authors to make their argument? Why or why not?

The Taliban Use Heroin as a Weapon Against US Soldiers

Gerald Posner

"[The Taliban] saw how heroin helped disable a foreign fighting force more than 20 years ago. And that lesson isn't lost on them."

Gerald Posner is chief investigative reporter for the news and commentary website the Daily Beast. In the following viewpoint he describes how the Taliban have used heroin as a tactical weapon against US troops. He suggests that the Taliban are taking Afghanistan's main cash crop—opium, from which the drug heroin is made—and introducing it to troops, many of whom have willingly turned to drugs as the boredom, horror, and length of the war eats away at them. Soldiers have even been turned into smugglers, with reports of some shipping packages home with drugs hidden cleverly inside. Posner says previous wars demonstrate the powerfully destabilizing effect drug addiction can have on armies. He urges army officials to become aware of the true extent of the heroin problem among their troops.

Forty years ago, the Vietnam War was partly undermined by heroin addiction among U.S. troops. Surely mindful of that, the Taliban and al Qaeda are now using Afghanistan's bountiful heroin supplies as a tactical weapon. An internal U.S. intelligence report has concluded that the two groups are targeting American troops in an effort to undermine their effectiveness, while raising cash to pay for new recruits and weaponry, a U.S. intelligence official tells The Daily Beast.

The Enemy Sees an Opportunity

It's a logical tactic. The drug is plentiful, cheap—less than $1 for a day's supply—and potent. And while Army officials publicly dismiss talk of any surging drug problem, some privately express concern about the possibility of increased drug use among bored and susceptible young soldiers.

According to the report, which the official spoke to me about only on the condition of anonymity, the Taliban and al Qaeda see an opportunity: U.S. and other NATO [North Atlantic Treaty Organization] soldiers are caught in an increasingly unpopular conflict with high stress and little to do in their spare time. Drugs are a tempting escape. The report cites the drug problems in previous drug-producing combat zones. In Vietnam, some frontline U.S. troop battalions had substance abuse rates that exceeded 20 percent, almost all due to China White, the almost-pure heroin from the adjacent Golden Triangle. Russian soldiers who served in Afghanistan in the 1980s returned to the motherland with an addiction rate that also approached 20 percent.

This heroin bomb then does collateral damage back home. The returning soldiers brought home a heroin problem to Russian cities that grew exponentially during the past two decades. This past March [2009], Russia's anti-narcotics bureau announced that the country had become the planet's "No. 1 heroin consumer."

Heroin Can Disable a Fighting Force

Today's Taliban-fighting Americans were yesterday's *mujahideen*-fighting Soviets. They saw how heroin helped disable a foreign fighting force more than 20 years ago. And that lesson isn't lost on them. With the Afghan opium crop at record levels—generating more than 90 percent of the global supply—and the Taliban and al Qaeda increasingly relying on the drug trade to finance their war, targeting U.S. soldiers also has the potential to seed new markets.

Officially, the subject remains taboo, especially given the [Barack] Obama administration's current debate about changing the Afghanistan military strategy. Barry McCaffrey, a retired four-star general who was the U.S. drug czar under [former president] Bill Clinton, told a conference of addiction-treatment providers that serious drug use among U.S. troops in Afghanistan has doubled in the last four years, and

British soldiers find a cache of Taliban heroin in the Helmand Province of Afghanistan. The viewpoint author believes that the Taliban want to get US and NATO soldiers hooked on heroin to reduce their combat effectiveness.

that as the Obama administration moves more soldiers from Iraq to Afghanistan, more will fall prey. "[Soldiers] are going to stick it up their nose and like it," he told the National Association of Addiction Treatment Providers this past May [2009].

The remarks went largely unnoticed, but Army officials were privately furious at McCaffrey's statements, telling me he didn't have the stats to back up his charge. But while Army officials talk a good game—arguing random drug testing is in place, the Army is now volunteers, not draftees, and the numbers of opiate addicts are still low—they are clearly concerned about what might be coming.

The Army's Response

In 2004, the military, worried even then about the huge supply of cheap opiates, began random drug testing of American troops in Iraq, and soon extended that to Afghanistan. Ten percent of troops in each unit are selected at random, once a month, for a urinalysis. But testing soldiers in a combat zone is not easy. Rhonda K. Paige, the chief of the public affairs and strategic communications office of the Army's deputy chief of staff, told The Daily Beast, "We apply the same testing requirements to soldiers in theater as we do to soldiers at home station; but not at the risk of the mission and/or our soldiers' personal safety."

George Wright, a Pentagon-based Army spokesman told me, "In Iraq, a majority of units inspected at the brigade, battalion, and company levels were meeting the intent of current Army policy, but compliance in Afghanistan is problematic due to operational tempo and unit dispersion."

Wright made a strong argument for the Army's many attempts to avoid the drug problems that afflicted troops in Vietnam, pointing out that it has aggressively trained soldiers to be better aware of the causes of drug abuse and "to erase the stigma associated with seeking behavioral health care." As for punishment for anyone who tested positive, Wright said, "Leaders will support soldiers to the highest degree possible, and will address each situation on its merits. However, substance abuse will not be tolerated in the Army. Every effort is made to help a soldier rehabilitate." That means that if somebody does test positive, the Army isn't likely to transfer out a combat soldier when it already has difficulty getting good fighting troops with experience on the front line.

Heroin "Was Everywhere"

"Through September 2006, [there were] no positive urinalysis results among deployed soldiers for heroin," he told me. He was not able to find any later data. But The Daily Beast spoke to six soldiers, four of whom had served in Iraq, and two from Afghanistan. All had developed opiate addictions and had sought treatment from the Veterans Hospitals in their home cities. None wanted to go on the record, because they were either in the Reserves, afraid their comments might be interpreted as criticism of the Army, or might reflect badly on their friends who were still serving honorably in the combat zones.

These six unanimously confirmed that heroin "was everywhere," especially in Afghanistan. Each of them also talked about local suppliers who had established pipelines into American troop installations in many parts of the countries. One, who had been based at the Bagram airfield, said that heroin was "sold at a lot of the shops in the bazaar" located just outside the air base's perimeter. They confirmed that some soldiers have bartered away military equipment, including knives, helmets, and flak jackets, for drugs. "Why do you think you can buy surplus Army equipment inside the bazaar," one solider asked me. (At Bagram, according to a written statement provided to *Salon* [an online magazine] by an Army spokesperson for the base, the "Military Police receive few reports of alcohol or drug issues.")

> **FAST FACT**
>
> Data compiled by the US military show that heroin use is on the rise among troops. In 2002 just 10 soldiers tested positive for heroin; by 2010, 116 had tested positive.

In conversations with Army officials, it becomes clear that the true extent of the heroin problem among American soldiers now serving in Afghanistan, and Iraq, is unknown. The military keeps statistics only on how many troops failed drug tests, as George Wright noted when he cited the zero-positive results in "deployed soldiers." But it turns out that that better information on long-term addiction comes not from the Army but from the U.S. Veterans Administration [VA].

Geographic Distribution of Heroin Users by Country

The United States has more than 1 million heroin users. Afghanistan is the source of much of the world's opium, from which heroin is made.

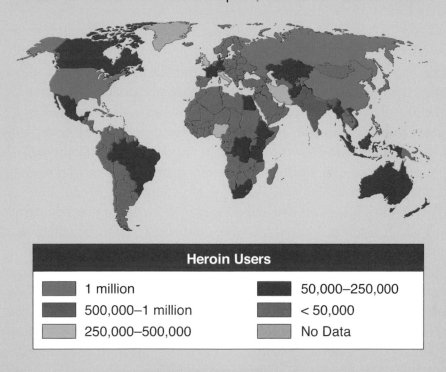

Heroin Users

- 1 million
- 500,000–1 million
- 250,000–500,000
- 50,000–250,000
- < 50,000
- No Data

Taken from: *The Global Afghan Opium Trade: A Threat Assessment.* United Nations Office on Drugs and Crime, July 2011.

According to reporting by Shaun McCanna in *Salon*, "The anecdotal information . . . suggests there may be a wave of new patients coming" to the VA. "Although they haven't shown up in the statistics yet, reports from methadone clinics suggest the VA's future patients may already be back in the States in force," McCanna reported.

"We're just starting to get a lot of Gulf War veterans," Dr. Jodie Trafton, a health-care specialist with the VA's Center for Health Care Evaluation in Menlo Park, California, told *Salon*, adding that young soldiers don't seek treatment unless urged to do so by their family.

When Soldiers Become Smugglers

But addiction is only one problem from having a fighting force stationed in the world's largest opium-producing nation. "I'd be astonished if we don't see soldiers who find 10 kilograms of heroin and pack it up in a birthday cake and send it home to their mother," McCaffrey said in May.

Army officials are still stinging over the 2005 incident in which four military intelligence soldiers, whose mission was to assist the Colombian government in surveillance and detection of drugs, transported more than 200 pounds of cocaine on military aircraft into Texas and Louisiana. They received general courts martial and the sergeant who was the ringleader got six years in prison. That was the same year that an Air National Guard pilot and a sergeant used a C-5 Galaxy military transport plane to sneak nearly 300,000 Ecstasy pills from Germany into New York. And in the past two years, the British have prosecuted nine soldiers for smuggling guns out of Iraq to trade for drugs and cash.

Army officials are not worried about large, far-flung narcotic cartels run by U.S. soldiers. Instead, they are concerned that some individuals may be tempted to make some fast and easy money. But the Army does not have the resources or ability to monitor every soldier who wants to earn a year's extra pay by mailing home a couple of packages of virtually pure heroin. The Daily Beast has learned that the DEA [Drug Enforcement Administration], which has the responsibility for developing major drug cases inside Afghanistan, does not have any American service personnel currently serving in Afghanistan or Iraq under a drug-related investigation.

This does not cover the more than 18,000 private armed security contractors, such as Blackwater and Armor Group, now working in those countries under Pentagon control. Some in the Afghan Ministry of Anti-Narcotics believe the private mercenaries might have more incentive and means to deal in heroin.

A senior DEA officer told me the agency is working hard to try to prevent heroin trafficking from Afghanistan becoming an American problem. "We're trying to build the complex cases to stop the [Colombian drug lord] Pablo Escobars of Afghanistan from getting a permanent foothold," he said. "We don't have the ability to stop every mom and pop dealer in a country where opium is the biggest cash crop. Some people are just going to fly under the radar."

The United States Should Buy Afghan Opium to Undermine the Taliban

Christopher Hitchens

"The best way to deprive the Taliban of drug profits? The United States should buy Afghanistan's poppy crop instead of trying to eradicate it."

The United States should buy Afghanistan's opium so the Taliban cannot sell it, argues Christopher Hitchens in the following viewpoint. He explains that the Taliban are kept in operation by the vast proceeds they earn from illegally selling heroin, which is made from the poppy plant. Hitchens suggests that the United States can cut into the Taliban's business by buying opium directly from Afghan farmers. Then, the United States could either turn it into legitimate medicines, or dispose of the crop. Either way, says Hitchens, the Taliban would be cut out of the loop, and the United States could prevent huge quantities of illegal drugs from ending up in global circulation. Hitchens says that the war in Afghanistan will not be won until the country's illicit drug trade is addressed, and he believes that the United States can accomplish several goals by buying it out from under the Taliban.

Before his death in 2011, Christopher Hitchens was a journalist and columnist for *Vanity Fair*.

AS YOU READ, CONSIDER THE FOLLOWING QUESTIONS:

1. What crop does Hitchens say Afghanistan exported thirty years ago?
2. Afghanistan produces what percentage of the world's opium, according to the author?
3. What is the United States in short supply of, according to Hitchens?

The best way to deprive the Taliban of drug profits? The United States should buy Afghanistan's poppy crop instead of trying to eradicate it.

I used to know Sir Sherard Cowper-Coles, [the British] ambassador in Kabul, and I have no reason to doubt that he was quoted correctly in the leaked cable from the deputy French ambassador to Afghanistan that has since appeared in the Parisian press. I think that he is right in saying that while there cannot be a straightforward "military victory" for the Taliban and other fundamentalist and criminal forces, nonetheless there is a chance that a combination of these forces can make the country ungovernable by the NATO [North Atlantic Treaty Organization] alliance. He may also be correct in his assertion that an increase of troops in the country might have unwelcome and unintended consequences, in that "it would identify us even more strongly as an occupation force and would multiply the targets" for the enemy.

If Afghanistan and Iraq have demonstrated one point over another, it is that the quantity theory of counterinsurgency is very unsoundly based. If a vast number of extra soldiers had been sent to Baghdad before the disastrously conducted war had been given a new strategy and a new command, then it would have been a case of staying in the same hole without ceasing to dig (and there would have been many more "body bags" as a consequence of the larger number of uniformed targets). As it is, we have learned so many lessons in Iraq

Why Do Afghans Grow Poppies?

A survey by the United Nations Office on Drugs and Crime revealed various reasons why Afghans decide to grow or not grow poppy plants, from which opium is made. Opium's high sale price was the number one reason.

Reasons for opium cultivation in 2011 in opium growing villages

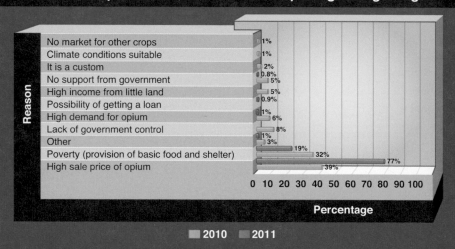

Taken from: *Afghanistan Opium Survey 2011*. United Nations Office on Drugs and Crime, January 2011, p. 8.

about how to defeat al-Qaida that we have the chance to apply them in Afghanistan. This is exactly the reverse of the glib and facile argument that used to counterpose the "good" Afghan war to the evil quagmire in Mesopotamia.

Afghanistan Is Nearly Lost

Speaking of quagmires, here are a few admittedly quantitative figures (taken from the testimony before Congress of Mark Schneider of the well-respected International Crisis Group). He quoted Adm. Mike Mullen of the Joint Chiefs of Staff as saying that suicide bombings in Afghanistan were up 27 percent in 2007 over 2006, commenting that

Mullen "should have added that they are up 600 percent over 2005, and that all insurgent attacks are up 400 percent over 2005." To darken the statistical picture further—this testimony was given last spring [2008]—one must also count the number of attacks on World Food Program convoys, on relief workers, and on prominent Afghan women. All of these show a steady upward curve, as does the ability of the Taliban to operate across the Pakistani border and to strike in the middle of the capital city as well as other cities, most notably its old stronghold of Kandahar. The final depressing figure is the index of civilian casualties caused by aerial bombardment from NATO forces: This year will show a large increase in these, as well, and that is one of the chief concerns underlying Sir Sherard's bleakly expressed view that the current U.S.-led strategy is "destined to fail."

Innumerable factors combine to constitute this depressing assessment, and many of them have to do with the sheer fact that Afghanistan, already extremely poor, scorched its own earth further in a series of civil wars and ethnic rivalries. I remember flying from Herat to Kabul on a U.N. [United Nations] plane a few years ago and being depressed by the rarity of even a splash of greenery in the mud-colored landscape. Thirty years ago, what was Afghanistan's most famous export? It was grapes, usually made into exceptionally fine raisins that were esteemed throughout the subcontinent. It was a country of vines and orchards. Now, even the vines and trees have mostly been cut down for firewood. Iraq could well be immensely rich in a decade or less: Afghanistan will be well-down even in "Third World" economic terms for a very long time to come.

FAST FACT

According to data reported in the *New York Times*, Afghanistan's opium industry was worth more than $6 billion between 2002 and 2012.

Opium Profits Keep the Taliban Alive

This is why it is peculiar of us, if not bizarre and quasi-suicidal, to insist that its main economic lifeblood continues to be wholly controlled by our enemies. The U.N. Office on Drugs and Crime [UNODC]

The UN Office of Drugs and Crime estimates that 193,000 hectares of Afghan poppy fields produce 93 percent of the world's opium. Some think that the United States would be better served in Afghanistan by buying the opium from the local Afghans so the money goes into the local economy and not to the Taliban.

tells us that last year [2007] Afghanistan's poppy fields, on 193,000 hectares of land, produced 93 percent of all the world's opium. The potential production could be as high as 8,200 metric tons. And, unsurprisingly, UNODC also reports that the vast bulk of the revenue from this astonishing harvest goes directly to the Taliban or to local warlords and mullahs. Meanwhile, in the guise of liberators, NATO forces appear and tell the Afghan villagers that they intend to burn their only crop. And the American embassy is only restrained by the Afghan government from pursuing a policy of actually spraying this same crop from the air! In other words, the discredited fantasy of [former US president] Richard Nixon's so-called "War on Drugs" is the dogma on which we are prepared to gamble and lose the country that gave birth to the Taliban and hospitality to al-Qaida.

Turn the Crop into Something Useful

Surely a smarter strategy would be, in the long term, to invest a great deal in reforestation and especially in the replanting of vines. While in the short term, hard-pressed Afghan farmers should be allowed to sell their opium to the government rather than only to the many criminal elements that continue to infest it or to the Taliban. We don't have to smoke the stuff once we have purchased it: It can be burned or thrown away or perhaps more profitably used to manufacture the painkillers of which the United States currently suffers a shortage. (As it is, we allow Turkey to cultivate opium poppy fields for precisely this purpose.) Why not give Afghanistan the contract instead? At one stroke, we help fill its coffers and empty the main war chest of our foes while altering the "hearts-and-minds" balance that has been tipping away from us. I happen to know that this option has been discussed at quite high levels in Afghanistan itself, and I leave you to guess at the sort of political constraints that prevent it from being discussed intelligently in public in the United States. But if we ever have to have the melancholy inquest on how we "lost" a country we had once liberated, this will be one of the places where the conversation will have to start.

EVALUATING THE AUTHOR'S ARGUMENTS:

Christopher Hitchens and Swaminathan S. Anklesaria Aiyar (author of the following viewpoint) disagree on whether buying Afghanistan's opium will drive the price up or down. After reading both viewpoints, which author do you think makes the better argument? Quote from the viewpoint in your answer.

Buying Opium Will Not Make Afghanistan's Drug Trade Unprofitable

Swaminathan S. Anklesaria Aiyar

In the following viewpoint, Swaminathan S. Anklesaria Aiyar argues that buying Afghanistan's opium is not the best way to make its drug trade unprofitable. He agrees that the Taliban profit from the drug trade but suggests that buying up the poppy crop (from which the drug heroin is made) will only make the drug more scarce and thus more lucrative. Indeed, he says, a more rare plant will sell for more money, helping the Taliban to make even more money. A better idea, says Aiyar, is to flood the market with opium. Excess amounts of any product are worth much less, and thus the Taliban will not be able to make as much profit. He suggests having neighboring Australia introduce so much poppy to the market that the plant—and its prized extracts—becomes worthless.

Swaminathan S. Anklesaria Aiyar, "Dump Opium in Afghanistan, Bankrupt Taliban." *Times of India,* February 20, 2011. Source: *The Times of India.* Copyright © 2011, Bennett, Coleman & Co. Ltd. All rights reserved. Reproduced by permission.

Aiyar is consulting editor of *Economic Times*. He has also served as a consultant to the World Bank and the Asian Development Bank.

AS YOU READ, CONSIDER THE FOLLOWING QUESTIONS:
1. Describe one approach to the Afghan drug trade the author thinks is "escapist."
2. What poppy extracts have legitimate medical uses, according to Aiyar?
3. What is the one country in which opium production is legal under government supervision, according to the author?

One reason for the Taliban's resilience in Afghanistan is the big money they make from the opium trade. Attempts to cut off external financing for the Taliban have failed since it generates so much money within the country.

The US has tried destroying the poppy crop. It has tried to use friendly mullahs to denounce opium as unIslamic. It has sought to promote grapes, saffron and high-yielding wheat as alternatives to poppy. None of these approaches has worked. In despair, some analysts want the US to buy the entire poppy crop in Afghanistan, and then destroy it.

Time for a New Approach
All these approaches are escapist, and fail to come to grips with ground realities. The Afghan government barely exists in much of the country, and many officials in rural areas are corrupt or in league with the Taliban. They cannot be depended on to destroy the poppy crop, not even with support from US helicopters. Many Afghans admit that drugs are unIslamic, but the profitability of poppy cultivation has easily overcome their moral scruples, especially since the damage is ultimately inflicted on white infidels in distant lands.

Since all proposed remedies so far have failed, we need to think out of the box and come up with a totally new approach. Forget any military or religious approach to the problem. Instead, let us understand what the laws of supply and demand imply in the opium context.

Afghanistan's Poppy Fields

By 2012 much of Afghanistan was engaged in opium cultivation.

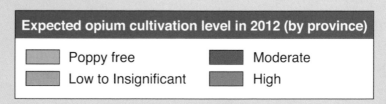

Expected opium cultivation level in 2012 (by province)

- Poppy free
- Low to Insignificant
- Moderate
- High

Taken from: Afghanistan Opium Survey 2012. United Nations Office on Drugs and Crime, April 2012, p. 5.

How Supply and Demand Can Help

To produce opium, Afghan farmers lance poppy plants, and painstakingly collect the latex that oozes out. The dried latex is called opium. It contains up to 12% morphine, along with codeine and alkaloids such as thebaine and nocapine. Morphine, codeine and other processed alkaloids have medical uses as painkillers. But drug lords process these alkaloids into heroin, and sell this highly addictive drug at sky-high prices on western streets.

Opium production is banned globally, save in India where it is produced on regulated farms under government supervision. Most opium production is illicit, and Afghanistan accounts for nine-tenths of it. The Taliban levy a tax on Afghan farmers and also buy opium to be processed and smuggled abroad.

Turkey was once a major opium producer, but banned it many years ago. Turkey and Australia now grow poppies under government regulation, but they do not use the manual route of lancing poppies and scraping off the ooze. Instead they mechanically harvest the entire poppy crop. This is called poppy straw, and it is then chemically processed to extract medical alkaloids like morphine.

Buying the Crop Will Not Work

Some international medical groups have complained that there is a global shortage of medical morphine, and that Africa in particular is condemned to needless pain for want of enough morphine. These groups believe the right approach is for the US to buy up the whole Afghan poppy crop and process this into morphine for medical use. Many hard-headed military and policy experts also think this can be an effective way of depriving the Taliban of opium income.

Problem: these experts are ignoring basic economics. Today, the Afghan poppy crop is grown mainly in southern provinces like Helmand. If the US or some medical council tries to buy up

FAST FACT

In 2012 the United Nations reported that only about 3.5 percent of the 375 tons of heroin that leaves Afghanistan every year is intercepted by authorities.

Helmand's poppy production, opium will become scarce in the black market and prices will skyrocket. This will induce other provinces to take up poppy cultivation. Indeed, cultivation will also spread rapidly to neighbouring countries (Iran, Pakistan, Turkmenistan, Uzbekistan and Tajikistan) and the resultant opium will be smuggled

Some think a better way to combat the opium trade in Afghanistan is to release so much opium onto the market that the price falls, making the crop almost worthless.

into Afghanistan. The Taliban will, of course, profit handsomely from this illicit trade.

Increasing Supply Makes It Less Profitable

Basic economics says that any strategy that makes opium scarce will fail, since it will encourage further cultivation. The solution lies in increasing the supply of opium so greatly that its price crashes, making cultivation unprofitable.

How can we achieve this? The US could ask Australia to licence a big jump in poppy straw production, guaranteeing to buy and process the entire production into opiates. These opiates could then be dumped in Afghanistan. Afghan opium prices will crash and farmers will turn to other crops.

Legalizing Drugs Can Work, Too

An alternative strategy could be for the US to legalize drug use. Once heroin becomes legal, its street price will plummet, and so will the Afghan price. However, political and religious opposition to legalizing drug use in the US is very strong. There will be much less opposition to dumping opiates in Afghanistan. Indeed, US farm belt legislators may even suggest poppy cultivation (with safeguards) in the US, providing farmers with a lucrative new crop.

EVALUATING THE AUTHOR'S ARGUMENTS:

Another suggestion Swaminathan S. Anklesaria Aiyar makes for decreasing the profitability of Afghanistan's drug trade is to legalize heroin. Then, he says, state governments can control the supply and the price, sidelining illegal markets like the one that funds the Taliban. What do you think of this suggestion? What problems might come with drug legalization? What benefits? List at least two pros and cons in your answer.

Chapter 3

How Should the United States Deal with the Taliban Going Forward?

Afghan president Hamid Karzai (center of photo) prepares to give a speech after being given a mandate by tribal elders and religious leaders to negotiate with the Taliban on June 4, 2010.

Viewpoint

1

Talking 'Bout Negotiation

Shamila N. Chaudhary

"As the United States plans to send troops home, what better time than now to turn to reconciliation."

Shamila N. Chaudhary is a South Asia analyst at the Eurasia Group and a senior fellow at the New America Foundation. She served as director for Pakistan and Afghanistan at the White House National Security Council from 2010 to 2011. In the following viewpoint, Chaudhary discusses five major reasons why critics think that talks with the Taliban will fail and why she thinks that the critics are wrong. Chaudhary deals with the deaths caused by the Taliban, their fundamentalism, their involvement with Pakistan, their ties with al Qaeda, and the issue of Karzai. The five major reasons against reconciliation reflect the ideological flaw of the war. However, since more killing is the alternative, reconciliation is the only way forward, says Chaudhary.

AS YOU READ, CONSIDER THE FOLLOWING QUESTIONS:

1. How many American soldiers have been killed since the war began in 2001?
2. What is the Karzai problem, according to the author?
3. What is the significance of Doha, the capital city of Qatar, in relation to the Taliban and Pakistan, according to the author?

The Obama administration has embarked on a fresh effort to get allies back on board with the goal of talks leading to Taliban reconciliation, following the Taliban's public acknowledgment of its willingness to negotiate. In a January 3 *statement*, the Taliban indicated they would establish a political office in Qatar that will be used "to come to an understanding with other nations." Does this mark one of the most historic developments since the beginning of the war: the Taliban shedding its status as an insurgency and beginning its transformation into a state? In another *statement* issued January 12, the Taliban reiterated its interest in increasing political efforts but added that this "does not mean a surrender from jihad and neither is it connected to an acceptance of the constitution of the stooge Kabul administration." So, which is it—talk or fight?

The Taliban's contradictory words offer little assurance of its willingness to follow through on commitments made through formal negotiations. But we should not interpret official statements as signs of agreement; the Taliban continues to face internal discord over the war, with a pro-reconciliation faction often operating in conflict with those still seeking military *victory*. Expect more schizophrenic statements from both the Taliban who *declared* victory on Jan. 15 and the United States, as both sides feel pressure to show strong negotiating positions.

Likewise, the U.S. approach of "fight, talk, build," does not mean that the administration speaks with one voice. The tensions among American defense, intelligence, and diplomatic communities on the Taliban's willingness to negotiate are *well documented*. At face value, the military's reluctance to characterize Taliban intentions reflects an unwillingness to acknowledge the failures of its military campaign in Afghanistan. The risk-averse nature of the intelligence community often lends itself to the most conservative estimate possible—rendering any possibility of negotiation impossible. Meanwhile, diplomats believe political talks are the only solution. The United States policy community remains stuck in an ideological debate over the Taliban's true identity: terrorist group, ideological movement, political entity, or insurgency? But time has run out for debates like this. Almost all parties, regardless of ideological bias or motivation, agree that talks are the only way out of Afghanistan.

If so, where do we go from here? How do we reconcile the major disagreements over reconciliation if it is the only way forward? There are five prominent and challenging reasons that officials and analysts use to say why negotiations can't or shouldn't work. Here's why they're wrong.

1. The Taliban Have Too Much Blood on Their Hands

Last week, Secretary Clinton *acknowledged* that the United States was considering transferring Guantanamo detainees to Qatar in exchange for talks with the Taliban. The deal would include former senior Taliban military commander Mullah Mohammed Fazl, implicated in *mass sectarian killings* prior to the 2001 U.S. invasion of Afghanistan. There's no debate that the Taliban's killing of Shiites is morally reprehensible. Furthermore, releasing a mass murderer to build trust for a peace process has been *criticized* by American analysts and Republican presidential hopefuls, not to mention Afghan and *regional stakeholders*. And that's for someone who's killed Afghans. The Taliban directly or indirectly killed more than 4,500 Americans.

According to the latest *estimates* from the Department of Defense, 1,761 members of the U.S. military died in Afghanistan as a result of the U.S. invasion, as well as 2,819 Americans killed in the Sept. 11 attacks, which al Qaeda leadership planned from the comfort of a Taliban-controlled Afghanistan. As Senator Dianne Feinstein *said*, "the Taliban is still a force to be reckoned with." Feinstein's remarks come on the heels of media reports on the U.S. National Intelligence Estimate on Afghanistan, which suggests little progress was made last year given the high number of casualties. Clinton would remind us that "*you don't negotiate with your friends.*" No one expects the United States will find immediate friendship from the likes of Mullah Fazl and other detainees if transferred, especially after years of confinement in Guantanamo. However, with death being the only constant of the

FAST FACT

More than 2,050 US troops (and 1,000 troops from other nations) have died fighting in Afghanistan since the war started in 2001.

past decade, we can only presume that they, like the United States, are looking for a way out of the fighting.

2. The Taliban Are Islamic Fundamentalists

Before losing power in December 2001, the Taliban were notorious for their human rights abuses, based on an interpretation of Islamic law that condoned public executions, the cutting off of hands as punishment for theft, death sentences for adultery, and extreme abuses of women. The Taliban's current position on these issues remains largely unknown—but suffice to say it's probably not changed much.

So far, it appears that U.S.-Taliban exploratory discussions are not contingent upon commitments to human rights standards or changes in religious ideology, focusing instead on detainee transfers and the establishment of an office in Qatar. But the question of whether the Taliban are too fundamentalist or too bound by ideology will eventually affect reconciliation discussions: It's clear that Afghan and U.S. stakeholders, not to mention domestic and international civil society, will not accept America negotiating with such a repressive organization. But the Taliban's religious fundamentalism is not the war the U.S. has chosen to fight. The Obama administration maintains its policy that the basis of the conflict and the core *goal* of the U.S. "must be to disrupt, dismantle, and defeat al Qaeda and its safe havens in Pakistan, and to prevent their return to Pakistan or Afghanistan." There is no mention of Taliban ideology—religious or otherwise—so it should not be the basis of negotiations. The United States will have to find other ways, possibly after negotiations, to influence issues such as human rights that will continue to be important to its values as a country and a government. But for now, the Taliban's Islamic fundamentalism is the straw man argument against reconciliation.

3. The Karzai Problem

President Hamid Karzai's inconsistent approach toward reconciliation continues to cause confusion, weaken confidence, and send the wrong messages. Even as the United States labeled its reconciliation policy as "Afghan-led" and announced its willingness to accept a Qatar-based Taliban office, Karzai *voiced* his opposition. Karzai's efforts to engage

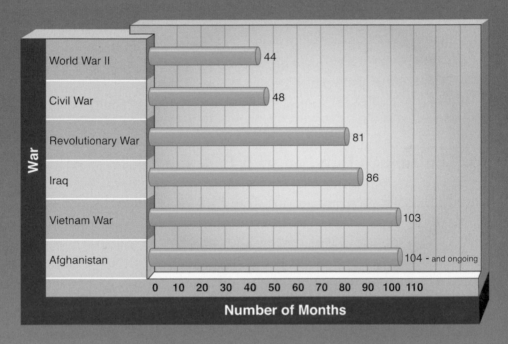

America's Longest War

In June 2010 the war in Afghanistan completed its 104th month, making it the longest war in US history. As of January 2013 it had gone on for 135 months.

War (vertical axis)

War	Number of Months
World War II	44
Civil War	48
Revolutionary War	81
Iraq	86
Vietnam War	103
Afghanistan	104 - and ongoing

Number of Months

Taken from: Rick Hampson, "Afghanistan: America's Longest War," *USA Today*, May 28, 2010.

Iran and India send mixed messages to the United States and Pakistan respectively, who respectively remain concerned about Iran and India's growing influence in Afghanistan. Potentially most debilitating is the Taliban's view of the Karzai government as a "puppet" administration.

Karzai's government has not completely ignored the Taliban. It is known for its willingness to engage former Taliban officials and established the High Peace Council for reconciliation. But by playing all sides at once, Karzai has neutralized his own negotiating power. Why? Karzai fears that the United States and the Taliban will abandon him once both sides get what they want out of negotiations. His fear of irrelevance is further triggered by the lack of discussion on his future role. Karzai publicly stated his intention to step down at the conclusion of his term in 2014, but *rumors abound* that he is exploring measures to extend his time in power. He also cannot neglect the need to define and secure his political legacy and ensure his future safety and comfort, and that of his family. Karzai's blessing will be critical for reconciliation; talks can feasibly move without him but not for long. The American side's top reconciliation diplomat, Marc Grossman, drove this point home after meeting with Karzai this weekend in Afghanistan, emphasizing any *formal peace talks* would be between Afghans.

As long as Karzai's in charge of Afghanistan, he will have a heavy hand in what reconciliation looks like. All interested parties—the Taliban, U.S., and even Afghanistan's neighbors—will have to keep up their charm offensive with Karzai if they want talks to go anywhere.

4. The Taliban Is in Bed with Pakistan

Yes, Pakistan supported the Taliban. Its policy of support began during the second government of Prime Minister Benazir Bhutto from 1993 to 1996. Bhutto tasked Interior Minister Gen. Nasirullah Babar with the responsibility of reopening routes to Central Asia through Afghanistan. Babar, credited as the "father of the Taliban," strengthened the Taliban movement with military, logistical, and technical support. In return, Pakistan's access to routes through Afghanistan became cheaper and easier, and it viewed strong ties with the Taliban government as a sufficient hedge against Indian influence.

Years later, after the Sept. 11 attacks and the U.S. invasion of Afghanistan in 2001, the Taliban leadership finds itself comfortably living in the safe haven of Pakistan. Or does it? If conditions were so comfortable and their presence so openly tolerated, the Taliban could easily set up a political office in Quetta, say, instead of Qatar, and proceed with negotiations from there. But the move to Doha represents the first public indication of the Taliban's true relationship with Pakistan—strategic and political but not ideological, a circumstance that ultimately allows for greater flexibility in reconciliation negotiations.

5. The Taliban Will Never Break Ties with al Qaeda

Those who think Taliban links to al Qaeda are too strong to be broken should know that Osama bin Laden moved to Afghanistan in 1996 at the invitation of a leader of the Northern Alliance—our (ahem) allies. Only after the Taliban assumed power did bin Laden develop an alliance with the fundamentalist government. For al Qaeda, the relationship with the Taliban is no more unique than its relations with other groups and individuals who benefit from offering the organization safe haven. They may agree ideologically on certain religious and political principles—both are Sunni-dominated groups who view the United States as an imperial force targeting Muslim countries. But after ten years of war, a clearly diminished al Qaeda leadership no longer offers the Taliban legitimacy for a potential return to Afghan political life. Rather, it is the United States, the Afghan government and people, and the international community.

The top five reasons for why reconciliation won't work are rooted in the one big reason why the war couldn't be won through military means: *it was ideologically flawed*. Reconciliation is going to be tough if we never agree on why we're fighting the war in the first place. But critics of reconciliation are not just being disagreeable; in their defense, they are being realistic. Reconciliation will not show immediate results—it may take years, even decades. For many of the governments involved, especially the United States, the war in Afghanistan has been one of urgency, where they must show tangible results to justify their involvement to constituents back home. In this spirit, as the United States plans to send troops home, what better time than now to turn to reconciliation, especially as the current outlook on security does not offer anything more tangible or immediate by way of success.

> ## EVALUATING THE AUTHOR'S ARGUMENTS:
>
> In this viewpoint Shamila N. Chaudhary argues that reconciliation talks with the Taliban are the only way out of Afghanistan. What do you think are her strongest and her weakest arguments? Support your views with evidence from the viewpoint.

The United States Should Not Negotiate with the Taliban

Amrullah Saleh

> "Negotiating with the Taliban after more than 10 years of fighting means giving legitimacy and space to militant extremism."

In the following viewpoint Amrullah Saleh, former head of the Afghan National Directorate of Security, argues that the United States should not negotiate with the Taliban. Over the last several years, the Taliban have used violence to become much stronger—given this, Saleh says, they are unlikely to be willing to negotiate any of their gains away. Not only will peace talks fail, but Saleh thinks they send the wrong message to the Afghan people. Negotiating with terrorists legitimizes their methods, he argues; engaging the Taliban in peace talks implies they are a respectable partner in peace, which Saleh insists they are not. Furthermore, even if the Taliban engage in peace talks, they are unlikely to give up their weapons, and Saleh says a peaceful Afghanistan hinges on a disarmed Taliban. For all of these reasons, he concludes it would be a mistake to negotiate with the

Amrullah Saleh, "Why Negotiate with the Taliban?," *Wall Street Journal,* February 10, 2012. Reprinted from the *Wall Street Journal* © 2012 Dow Jones & Company. All rights reserved.

Taliban—doing so would undo the progress that has been made in the country to this point.

AS YOU READ, CONSIDER THE FOLLOWING QUESTIONS:
  1. What, according to Saleh, now "seems like a dream"?
  2. What advantages does the author say the Taliban have gained?
  3. What do the Afghan people think of the Taliban, according to Saleh?

Washington's olive branch to the Taliban—no matter the excuses or justifications—amounts to the management of failure, not the mark of victory. Negotiating with the Taliban after more than 10 years of fighting means giving legitimacy and space to militant extremism.

The objective of NATO's [North Atlantic Treaty Organization's] post-9/11 intervention in Afghanistan was to starve militant extremism by defeating the nexus of al Qaeda and the Pakistan-backed Taliban. That now seems like a dream.

With support from Pakistan, the Taliban has managed to protract the fighting and create a strategic deadlock. The U.S. military surge in 2010 weakened the Taliban, but it hardly pressured their strategic support across the Durand line in Pakistan. So the deadlock remains—chiefly because of Pakistan's unwillingness to cooperate fully with NATO, coupled with the fractured state of Afghan politics since the fraud-marred 2009 presidential elections.

Pakistan and the Taliban have no interest in producing quick positive results from talks. The Taliban has already gained certain advantages, including the possible transfer or release of their commanders from U.S. custody, the opening of an office in Qatar, and the legitimacy to enter into mainstream politics at the time of their choosing. They will definitely use these preliminary gains to further their psychological influence over the Afghan populace. And they won't likely bargain away the gains they have earned by suicide bombings, ambushes and the marginalization of civil society. Now that the Taliban has guaranteed its basic survival, it will fight for domination.

Talks Would Undermine Legitimate Leaders

Washington's talks with the Taliban—taking place, on and off, in Qatar—come at a time when most anti-Taliban Afghan civil-society leaders have deserted President Karzai. He is head of a heavily subsidized state whose pay master (Washington) is now largely bypassing his government to negotiate with the enemy. This raises the question: Who and what does President [Hamid] Karzai represent?

In a bid to make himself relevant, President Karzai has adopted a strategy of meddling. He has demanded that NATO halt night raids, hand over the Bagram detention facility, and place strict restrictions on security companies. He has also refused to echo NATO's mission goals and justifications, and he wanted the Taliban to open an office in Saudi Arabia, not Qatar.

> ## FAST FACT
>
> The Congressional Research Office estimates the war in Afghanistan cost the United States $443 billion in its first decade (between 2001 and 2011).

In return, NATO has accused Mr. Karzai of corruption, of committing abuses of human rights, and of being detached from reality. Successful counterinsurgency work requires international troops and the host nation to be seen as unified; that is simply not the case here. Pakistan and the Taliban are more coordinated in their approaches than are NATO and Afghanistan.

This is one of the key reasons why concerned anti-Taliban Afghans are creating a third force to ensure their rights and interests are represented and protected. They no longer see either President Karzai or NATO committed to those rights and interests. Though fragmented in their approach, these forces share a common goal: to counterbalance the growing influence of the Taliban and to fill the vacuum created by the declining relevance of Afghanistan's democratic institutions.

Talks Will Not Bring Stability

Certainly no Afghan political coalition can stop Washington from talking to the Taliban—but those talks won't bring stability. Talks and a potential ceasefire may provide the U.S. and its NATO allies

their justification for a speedy withdrawal, but it won't change the fundamentals of the problem in Afghanistan. Striking a deal with the Taliban without disarming them will shatter the hope of a strong, viable, pluralistic Afghan state.

The absolute majority of the Afghan people are against the Taliban and the domination of our country by militant extremism. They have wholeheartedly supported and participated in the democratic process, but they are now marginalized both by President Karzai, who controls massive resources with no accountability, and the international community, which is focused disproportionately on transition, withdrawal and the Taliban.

Talks Would Endanger the Entire Mission

Afghanistan's neglected majority can provide a political alternative for the military mission in Afghanistan. Its inclusion, which the U.S. could secure by pursuing reconciliation in a way that pressures President Karzai to respect the role of parliament and independent judges, would contain or push back the Taliban, increase the cost of war for Pakistan, and provide hope for post-transition Afghanistan.

Former Afghan intelligence chief Amrullah Saleh warns that President Hamid Karzai's strategy of reconciliation with the Taliban is dangerous for the country.

By contrast, should that majority remain outside the strategic calculus, we'll see further fragmentation of political power and legitimacy in Afghanistan. That will weaken Washington's position and endanger the entire mission.

EVALUATING THE AUTHOR'S ARGUMENTS:

Amrullah Saleh argues that negotiating with the Taliban legitimizes violence and undoes progress made in Afghanistan. Shamila N. Chaudhary (author of the previous viewpoint) argues that negotiating with the Taliban is the most reasonable way to end the long war that everyone wants to be over. After reading both viewpoints, which author do you think makes the stronger argument? Why? List at least two pieces of evidence that sway you.

Taliban Fighters Can Be Convinced to Lay Down Their Weapons

"Reintegration programs are a core element of peace-building processes in conflict-affected countries around the world."

Mark Sedra

In the following viewpoint Mark Sedra argues that reintegration programs can help end the war in Afghanistan. He explains that many Taliban fighters side with the Taliban because they are paid to do so— some receive more money than they would if they worked for the Afghan police. Sedra suggests offering such people money, job training, and other forms of assistance can make siding with the Taliban less attractive to them. With plenty of people willing to fight, the Taliban see no reason to end the war or come to the negotiating table, explains Sedra. But if their supply of fighters can be paid to switch sides, the Taliban will be critically weakened. He therefore thinks reintegration programs must be part of any end to the war in Afghanistan.

Sedra is a research scholar in Canada's University of Waterloo Political Science Department.

Perhaps the most significant news to come out of the London Conference on Afghanistan held on January 28th [2010] was the announcement by President [Hamid] Karzai that the Afghan Government, with donor funding, was establishing a reintegration program for Taliban members willing to renounce violence. It was part of a number of moves, including the de-listing of five former Taliban members from the UN's [United Nations'] terrorist blacklist, intended to lure the Taliban leadership to the bargaining table.

Making a Reintegration Program Work

This is not completely new ground for the Afghan government, which established by Presidential decree in May 2005 a National Independent Peace and Reconciliation Commission, which sought to drive so-called moderate Taliban away from the movement in exchange for some limited incentives. The program largely failed due to a meager budget, which prevented it from offering credible incentives (not more than bus fare in some cases), and inadequate vetting and monitoring systems to prevent Taliban imposters from benefiting from the program. According to some observers, the majority of the beneficiaries of the program were common criminals rather than Taliban fighters. While funding won't be a problem for this new reintegration scheme with the international community agreeing to the establishment of a $500 million trust fund—approximately $140 million has already been committed to it—preventing fraud will pose a challenge. The reality is that the Taliban don't carry ID cards, and conducting background checks on up to 10,000 potential beneficiaries will strain the intelligence gathering capacity of the Afghan government. Nonetheless, the very fact that the donor community has bought into this latest plan, unlike earlier schemes, bodes well for the program's future.

Clarifying Misperceptions

While there is an emerging consensus among key stakeholders and observers that the reintegration program is a positive step, it has received mixed reviews in the Western press and public opinion. In one interview I gave to one of the main Canadian TV networks on the subject, I was asked whether it was "a good idea to give cash pay-outs to terrorists"? This statement typifies existing misperceptions about the proposed program. While the program's finer details have yet to

Taliban fighters in Kandahar, Afghanistan, turn in their weapons as part of President Hamid Karzai's Taliban reconciliation program. Upon agreeing to participate in the peace initiative, the insurgents will be reintegrated into Afghan society.

be released, and the proof will most certainly be in the fine print, two key points have to be clarified:

1. The program will not offer cash payouts to Taliban members. Rather it will provide assistance for those who renounce violence to reintegrate into the civilian economy. This can include vocational training, job placement, micro-credit, or agricultural packages in the form of tools, seeds etc. . . . This assistance is in line with the support provided to former Northern Alliance fighters between 2003 and 2006 under the auspices of the Afghan New Beginnings Programme, a UNDP [United Nations Development Programme]–administered disarmament, demobilization and reintegration program that demobilized over 63,000 former combatants.

2. The main focus of the program is not that hardcore, ideologically motivated Taliban with links to al-Qaeda and other global jihadi [Muslim religious warriors] groups, but the lower level, rank-and-file members who fight for a daily wage (often exceeding that paid to the Afghan security forces) to support their families.

A Good First Step

The program is a first step in a broader political process, based on the fundamental realization that there is no military solution to the Afghan con-

FAST FACT

North American Treaty Organization (NATO) major general David Hook said that as of July 2012, 4,946 former Taliban members had joined reintegration programs, which require them to cease fighting.

flict. The hope is that by drying up the Taliban's supply of occasional fighters and foot soldiers, while simultaneously exerting increased military pressure on it via the U.S. troop surge, you can compel the leadership (the Quetta Shura) to compromise, something it has been unwilling to consider due to the not unreasonable belief that it is winning. To achieve this broader goal of a political settlement President Karzai has requested the support of the Saudi King and Pakistani government, two powers that have historically exercised significant influence over the Taliban leadership.

The Taliban's Growing Reach

The Taliban have taken control of increasingly larger parts of Afghanistan. Some policy makers think one way to rob the Taliban of their foot soldiers is to give them job training and cash incentives.

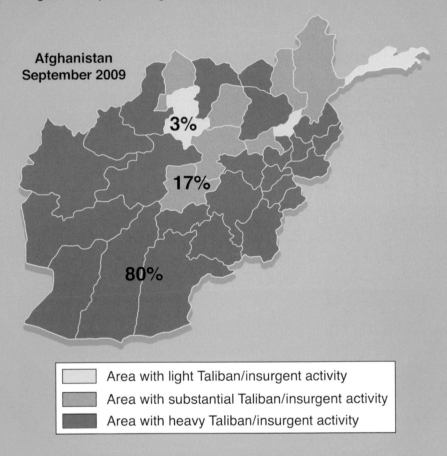

Afghanistan
September 2009

3%

17%

80%

Area with light Taliban/insurgent activity

Area with substantial Taliban/insurgent activity

Area with heavy Taliban/insurgent activity

Taken from: Marc W. Herold. "The Obama/Pentagon War Narrative, the Real War and Where Afghan Civilian Deaths Do Matter." Universidad de Granada, 2012, and the International Council on Security and Development, 2009.

Many Afghan civil society organizations, particularly women's groups and human rights advocacy organizations, have (quite reasonably) expressed strong reservations over the prospect of any compromise with the Taliban, fearing a return to the draconian rule of the Taliban period. Here I think the government must be clear that any negotiation with the Taliban will have clear red lines, and those lines can be found in the Afghan constitution, which provides strong protections for fundamental rights and freedoms.

A Core Element of Peace

The hurdles facing a Taliban reintegration scheme are significant, from problems with vetting and monitoring to security concerns. However, it is crucial for the establishment of a sustainable peace. Reintegration programs are a core element of peace-building processes in conflict-affected countries around the world from East Timor to Sierra Leone. Facilitating the return of combatants into civilian society is part of the wider process of reconciliation. While many citizens in NATO [North Atlantic Treaty Organization] states may find the idea of providing incentives to enemies who may have killed or wounded their own distasteful, without such a gesture the war could continue indefinitely. Making the decision to sue for peace is often more difficult than opting to continue fighting due to deep feelings of grievance on all sides, but if the Afghan insurgency has taught us anything over the past eight years, it is the only route to stability.

EVALUATING THE AUTHOR'S ARGUMENTS:

In this viewpoint Mark Sedra uses facts, examples, and reasoning to argue that Taliban fighters can be convinced to lay down their weapons. He does not, however, use any quotations to support his point. If you were to rewrite this article and insert quotations, what authorities might you quote from? Where would you place them, and why?

Taliban Fighters Are Unlikely to Lay Down Their Weapons

Ben Farmer

"'It's all just for show, it's nothing. These people are told to show up with a few old guns so it looks like a success.'"

Efforts to get Taliban fighters to lay down their weapons are unlikely to work, explains Ben Farmer in the following viewpoint. He says that many of the insurgents who have signed up for Afghanistan's reintegration program—which gives them money, job training, and other incentives if they leave the Taliban—take the money, even as they stay loyal to the Taliban. Others are common criminals who were never associated with the Taliban, and just want money. Farmer presents evidence that indicates a large amount of the money spent on convincing Taliban fighters to lay down their weapons has been wasted or been spent on the wrong people.

Since 2008 Farmer has been the Afghanistan correspondent for the *Sunday Telegraph,* a prominent London newspaper.

Wrapped in shawls against the cold, some with scarves to hide their faces, the men stand in front of a table bearing an arsenal of assault rifles and rockets.

As the insurgents renounce their armed struggle and declare they have made peace with Hamid Karzai's government, local journalists film the ceremony for the evening television.

Such scenes are now a common feature of Afghan news bulletins and portray one of the main pillars of NATO's [North Atlantic Treaty Organization's] strategy to overpower the Taliban and force them to the negotiating table prior to the planned exit by US and British forces.

However, *The Sunday Telegraph* has discovered disturbing evidence that all is not as it seems.

Imposters Seek Cash Handouts

New figures have now shown that over the last 18 months the "reintegration" scheme which Britain has funded with £7 million has attracted only 19 militants in Helmand province, where British troops are fighting.

And in at least one Afghan province, the insurgents pledging to change their ways and uphold the Afghan constitution were not what they seemed, officials have disclosed.

Some 200 insurgents in the northern province of Sar-e Pol have recently been struck off the programme, officials told *The Sunday Telegraph*, because checks subsequently found they were not genuine fighters but instead imposters seeking cash handouts.

The news will not surprise the scheme's sceptics who allege that Western tax-payers are being duped by criminals, the unemployed and corrupt local officials while the real fighters stay in the conflict, or only join the government temporarily.

Taliban Fighters Remain Committed

A leaked NATO report earlier this month [February 2012] also appeared to cast doubt on the very premise of the reintegration programme—that Taliban fighters are tired, motivated by money and want a way out.

Interrogators who have questioned thousands of insurgent prisoners in the past year reported instead that they remain motivated, feel their support is rising and their victory inevitable as foreign troops withdraw.

Fighters in Helmand, where the great majority of Britain's 397 dead have been killed, remain too afraid of their comrades in the Taliban to publicly relinquish the struggle and join the scheme despite security gains in the province, NATO and Afghan officials said.

Under the scheme, agreed two years ago at the London conference on Afghanistan, fighters are offered amnesty, training, jobs and aid for their villages if they leave the insurgency.

Around 3,000 men have joined nationwide in the past 18 months, but figures show the take-up in the southern and eastern strongholds of Taliban support, including in Helmand where Britain has been fighting for six years, has been negligible compared to that in the relatively peaceful north.

A Partial Picture

NATO officers insist that the low figures do not reflect the unknown number of fighters who are quietly laying aside their weapons without publicity and settling their differences with Hamid Karzai's government.

Major General David Hook, the British officer who leads NATO support for the Afghanistan Peace and Reintegration Programme (APRP), said the numbers painted only a partial picture.

"They don't want to come in, because they are afraid that coming in to us exposes them to the threat of the Taliban," he told *The Sunday Telegraph*. "At the moment some of them are more afraid of the Taliban than they are of being killed or captured.

"The question here is how many people have done what Afghans traditionally do when they get tired of fighting. They have just gone home, laid their weapons aside and gone back to normal society. This informal effect is difficult to measure."

Incidence Rates by Race

Tens of thousands of combatants have been disarmed and given job training, money, or other incentives to stay out of the fight. It is unclear, though, how many of these people fought with the Taliban or whether they have truly ceased insurgent activity.

Disarmament, Demobilization, and Reintegration in Afghanistan

Time Frame	Duration	Total Disarmed	Total Demobilized
October 1, 2003–July 31, 2005	22 months	63,380	62,376

Reintegration Options

Option	Participants
Agriculture	24,160
Vocational training and job placement	13,253
Small business	14,687
De-mining	1,102
Afghan National Army (ANA) or Police (ANP)	ANA: 761 / ANP: 105
Contracting teams	501
Teacher training	462
Other	773
Not participating	2,659
Total	55,804

Taken from: United Nations Disarmament, Demobilization, and Reintegration Resource Centre. "Country Programme: Afghanistan." www.unddr.org/countryprogrammes.php?o=121 (accessed March 23, 2011).

British commanders point to lower levels of violence in districts such as Nad-e Ali as proof that fighters must be relinquishing the fight. But critics say the scheme is not working where it is most needed.

Pressure to End the War

Pressure for a breakthrough is likely to increase as the 2014 deadline for withdrawal of international combat troops approaches, increasing anxiety over how the Afghan security forces will hold up when in charge.

Politicians in the US and elsewhere—in several cases facing imminent elections—are under pressure to speed the drawdown of troops.

Leon Panetta, the US defence secretary, said last week [early February 2012] he wanted America to switch to mainly training missions by the middle of next year, and France has promised to hasten its exit as [President] Nicholas Sarkozy faces a tough presidential election campaign this spring. [Editor's note: Sarkozy lost the election.]

Diplomatic efforts have focused on trying to open channels to the Taliban's ruling council, most recently by agreeing to a political office in Qatar, in the hope of one day helping Mr Karzai's government reach a political deal or "grand bargain".

Envoys in Kabul hope tentative talks may begin within weeks in the Gulf State [i.e., Qatar], though even the most optimistic stress any resulting peace process would probably take years.

Marc Grossman, American special envoy to Afghanistan and Pakistan, reportedly met Taliban negotiators in Qatar late last month [January 2012].

One of the most imminent obstacles he faces is a Taliban demand that five of their leaders are transferred from Guantanamo Bay prison [US military detention camp in Cuba], where they have been held for a decade, as a confidence-building measure.

Mr Grossman has said no decision has been made, but the concession faces growing resistance from American congressmen.

"The Same Men Each Week"

At the other end of the scale, the APRP and Maj Gen Hook aim to weaken the insurgency by drawing away lowly fighters motivated more by unemployment and local grievances than ideology, or who are weary after years of fighting.

Donors have set up a trust fund of £92 million, including £7 million from Britain, to fund it.

The money pays for Afghan officials to reach out to fighters in their area and then provide a monthly stipend of around £100 as well as training and jobs to those who want to settle, plus aid to their villages.

Such reintegration is unlikely until a broader peace deal is reached, some critics argue. Fighters will not defect piecemeal until their comrades also stop fighting and they are free from the threat of reprisal, their argument goes.

Maj Gen Hook disagrees, saying the two approaches feed off each other.

"The more we can integrate, the more we undermine the coherence of the various organisations, the more likely we are to have talks, because we are taking the wind from their sails," he explained.

Another fear is that those joining the scheme are either not real fighters, or are only joining temporarily to gain a respite from the coalition surge.

Such concerns stem from memories of similar reintegration ceremonies in the late 1980s when Najibullah, the Soviet-backed president, tried to persuade the Mujahideen to give up their struggle, often with large sums of money.

A running joke at the time was that the same men could be seen handing in their weapons each week.

Taliban Fighters or Common Criminals?

Maj Gen Hook rejects the possibility the same is still happening and said greater vetting had been brought in. Anyone wanting to join the scheme is now verified locally and then again by Afghan defence and security officials in Kabul.

Eye and fingerprint scans are taken so they cannot try re-joining later on.

He admits the rush to set up the scheme had caused problems at first and it was still "of variable quality".

But the programme was now running at "warp speed", he said, and the 200 Sar-e Pol cases proved new vetting checks were weeding out fakes.

He said: "Because we hadn't established a proper vetting process, they were all accepted into the programme and for the past nine to

Marc Grossman, American special envoy to Afghanistan and Pakistan, met with Taliban negotiators in Qatar in January 2011.

ten months, it's been a constant issue, because when we vetted them nationally, we realised that they weren't all bona fide insurgents.

"The double vetting has been to take away stuffing the programme with local cronies and to make sure that the people who come in are insurgents and not just common criminals, which was I think a justifiable criticism at the start of the programme." The Sar-e Pol imposters had not been given any of the £100 per month allowance, he said.

"I am reasonably confident the Afghans have a robust process because they turn people away all the time," he added.

"It's All Just for Show"

Syed Anwar Ahmadti, governor of Sar-e Pol, said more than 600 insurgents had joined the government in his province in the past year and confirmed that 200 had subsequently been judged fraudulent.

He however disagrees with that ruling, made in Kabul, and believes that the men had been fighting the government. The decision not to pay them will discourage others from laying aside their weapons, he said.

"It doesn't matter if they don't have guns, they were helping the insurgency in logistics or some other capacity, without guns." Sceptics allege the "insurgents" are in some cases only local men who are rounded up and given old weapons to hand in, so that local officials can appear efficient while also raking off a share of the reintegration money.

Syed Obadullah Sadat, a council member from the eastern province of Ghazni has publicly denounced a defection last month by more than a dozen fighters as a sham.

He said: "The process is fake, people are doing it for money. It's all just for show, it's nothing. These people are told to show up with a few old guns so it looks like a success."

Dr Ghani Bahadari, the Afghan official in Ghazni who runs the scheme, rejected the criticism as "gossip".

He said: "The reason they joined the government is that their leaders have established an office in Qatar and showed their interest in peace. They have also told us they are tired of war."

EVALUATING THE AUTHOR'S ARGUMENTS:

Ben Farmer quotes from several sources to support the points he makes in his viewpoint. Make a list of everyone he quotes, including their credentials and the nature of their comments. Then, analyze his sources—are they credible? Are they well qualified to speak on this subject? What specific points do they support?

Facts About the Taliban

Editor's note: These facts can be used in reports to add credibility when making important points or claims.

The Taliban's History
The Taliban came to power in Afghanistan in 1994. By 1996 they controlled Kabul, the nation's capital.

Draconian laws based on a strict interpretation of Islam were a main feature of their rule. According to the Revolutionary Association of the Women of Afghanistan (RAWA), banned activities included
- listening to music
- watching movies and television
- celebrating non-Islamic Afghan holidays, such as the new year and Labor Day
- shaving one's beard
- keeping pigeons or other birds
- kite flying
- clapping during sporting events
- reading non-Islamic books or magazines
- using the Internet

Afghans were forced to
- change any non-Islamic names to Islamic ones
- get certain kinds of haircuts
- wear Islamic clothing and an Islamic hat at all times
- pray at least five times a day in a mosque
- wear a turban if they wanted to attend school

Many laws were aimed at women. Women were not allowed to
- hold most jobs outside the home (including as teachers, engineers, and most other professional posts), and only a few female doctors and nurses were allowed to work in certain hospitals and could only attend to female patients

- drive cars
- leave their homes unless accompanied by a father, brother, or husband
- purchase items directly from male shopkeepers
- be attended by male doctors, even in an emergency
- go to school, university, or any other nonreligious institution
- be seen outdoors in anything but a burqa, a restrictive garment that completely covers them save only a screen for their eyes—if even a part of their ankle was exposed they could be whipped
- use cosmetics; women who dared to paint their fingernails could have their fingers cut off.
- touch even the hand of a man they were not related to
- wear shoes that could produce a sound while walking (such as shoes with heels)
- laugh loudly
- play sports
- ride bicycles (even with a male chaperone)
- wear brightly colored clothing, even under a burqa
- wear pants with flared legs, even under a burqa
- gather together, even in someone's home
- appear on the balconies of their own homes
- appear in the windows of their own houses (house windows were required to be tinted, so women could not be seen from the street)
- appear in photographs

Taliban leader Mullah Muhammad Omar formed a relationship with al Qaeda terrorist leader Osama bin Laden when Bin Laden came to Afghanistan in 1996, seeking a place where he could develop his ideology, train followers, and plot terrorist attacks.

Al Qaeda executed the largest of these attacks on September 11, 2001, when nineteen al Qaeda–trained terrorists hijacked four airplanes and flew them into buildings and other areas in the United States, killing nearly three thousand Americans.

In the wake of the attacks, the United States demanded the Taliban hand over Bin Laden so he could be brought to justice.

The Taliban refused, and so the United States (along with troops from other countries) invaded Afghanistan in October 2001.

The Taliban were quickly removed from power, but many members remained in the country.

For the next twelve years, Taliban members conducted a persistent insurgency, attacking US and international troops, Afghan government officials, international embassies, and other targets wherever they were able.

The US war effort ebbed and flowed over this time period. The US lost focus in Afghanistan when it invaded Iraq in 2003. For the next several years, many military resources and troops were devoted to the war in Iraq rather than the one in Afghanistan.

As a result, by 2009 the Taliban had regained control of critical areas of Afghanistan.

President Barack Obama thus sent a "surge" of thirty-three thousand additional troops to the region, which helped forces regain control of some of these areas.

It remains to be seen whether all American troops will be withdrawn by 2014, as they are slated to be.

American Opinions of the Taliban

A March 2012 poll taken jointly by NBC News and the *Wall Street Journal* asked Americans whether they thought the war in Afghanistan against the Taliban (and the terrorist group al Qaeda) had been very successful, somewhat successful, somewhat unsuccessful, or very unsuccessful. The poll revealed that
- 9 percent said the war was very successful;
- 48 percent said somewhat successful;
- 23 percent said somewhat unsuccessful;
- 18 percent said very unsuccessful; and
- 2 percent were unsure.

A CBS News survey taken between September and October 2011 asked Americans about their long-term view of US military operations in Afghanistan. The survey found that

- 39 percent thought the United States was right to remove the Taliban from power and stay in Afghanistan to help stabilize the country;
- 32 percent thought the United States was right to remove the Taliban from power but then should have left Afghanistan soon after that;
- 24 percent thought the United States should have never gotten involved in Afghanistan in the first place; and
- 5 percent were unsure.

US forces killed al Qaeda leader Osama bin Laden in May 2011. Shortly after that event, CBS News polled Americans on whether they thought Bin Laden's death was cause for the United States to leave Afghanistan. Responses were that

- 20 percent of Americans said US troops should leave Afghanistan because Bin Laden's death indicated that the Taliban are less of a threat and our presence there is no longer necessary;
- 72 percent said the United States should keep troops in Afghanistan because the Taliban still remain a threat;
- 3 percent said it depends; and
- 5 percent were unsure.

A poll taken by the Pew Research Center between March and April 2011 found that

- 10 percent of Americans thought that in the long run it was very likely that Afghanistan will become a country that is stable enough to withstand the threat posed by the Taliban and other groups;
- 39 percent thought this was somewhat likely;
- 29 percent thought this was not too likely;
- 16 percent thought this was not at all likely; and
- 5 percent were unsure.

A May 2009 CNN/Opinion Research Corporation poll found that

- 73 percent of Americans said that if the Taliban or members of al Qaeda deposed the Pakistani government and took power in that country, it would cause major problems for the United States;

- 24 percent said such an event would cause minor problems for the United States;
- 3 percent said it would cause no problems for the United States;
- 1 percent were unsure;
- 59 percent said they would favor sending US ground troops into Pakistan if it seemed likely that the Taliban or members of al Qaeda would depose the Pakistani government;
- 38 percent said they would oppose such an action; and
- 3 percent were unsure.

A December 2009 poll conducted jointly by NBC News and the *Wall Street Journal* found that
- 42 percent of Americans worried that the United States will invest a lot of money and American lives in the war in Afghanistan and have little to show for it;
- 48 percent of Americans worried that the United States will not do enough to deal with the threat of al Qaeda and the Taliban in Afghanistan, and will be more vulnerable as a result;
- 10 percent were unsure;
- 9 percent of Americans thought it was "definitely right" to send an additional thirty thousand troops to Afghanistan in 2009, with plans to withdraw them around 2011;
- 35 percent thought this plan was "probably right";
- 20 percent thought this plan was "probably wrong";
- 21 percent thought this plan was "definitely wrong"; and
- 13 percent did not know enough about the situation to express an opinion.

A December 2009 poll by CNN found that
- 66 percent of Americans thought it was unlikely that Afghanistan will have a democratic government that will not be overthrown by terrorists or the Taliban;
- 33 percent thought it was likely that Afghanistan will have a democratic government that will not be overthrown by terrorists or the Taliban; and
- 1 percent were unsure.

Organizations to Contact

The editors have compiled the following list of organizations concerned with the issues debated in this book. The descriptions are derived from materials provided by the organizations. All have publications or information available for interested readers. The list was compiled on the date of publication of the present volume; the information provided here may change. Be aware that many organizations take several weeks or longer to respond to inquiries, so allow as much time as possible for the receipt of requested materials.

Afghan Women Network (AWN)
Karta Parwan Square, House #22
Kabul, Afghanistan
website: www.afghanwomennetwork.af

AWN is the only umbrella entity for women/gender-based organizations in Afghanistan. It comprises seventy-two organizations and three thousand members in both Pakistan and Afghanistan. AWN is a nongovernmental organization that works to empower Afghan women and ensure their equal participation in Afghan society.

Afghan Women's Organization
789 Don Mills Rd., Ste. #312
Toronto, ON M3C 1T5
Canada
(416) 588-3585
website: www.afghanwomen.org

This organization was created to address the unique needs of Afghan women and children in the Greater Toronto Area and even as far as Afghanistan and Pakistan. It is dedicated to assisting Afghan women in all aspects of integration and adaptation to Canadian life; encouraging and motivating Afghan women to participate in and contribute to life in Canada; encouraging and promoting skill-building and development among Afghan women; developing a community support network for women; promoting English language development; and organizing and implementing programs to educate and empower young Afghans to cope with personal, cultural, and social issues.

American Enterprise Institute (AEI)
1150 Seventeenth St. NW, Washington, DC 20036
(202) 862-5800 • fax: (202) 862-7177
website: www.aei.org

AEI is a scholarly research institute that is dedicated to preserving limited government, private enterprise, and a strong foreign policy and national defense. It publishes books, including *Democratic Realism: An American Foreign Policy for a Unipolar World,* and *The Islamic Paradox: Shiite Clerics, Sunni Fundamentalists, and the Coming of Arab Democracy*; and a bimonthly magazine, *American Enterprise.*

The Brookings Institution
1775 Massachusetts Ave. NW, Washington, DC 20036
(202) 797-6000 • fax: (202) 797-6004
e-mail: brookinfo@brook.edu
websites: www.brookings.org; www.brookings.edu

The institution, founded in 1927, is a think tank that conducts research and education in foreign policy, economics, government, and the social sciences. In 2001 it began America's Response to Terrorism, a project that provides briefings and analysis to the public and that is featured on the center's websites. It publishes the quarterly *Brookings Review,* the periodic *Policy Briefs,* and books on troubled countries, including Afghanistan.

Center for Strategic and International Studies (CSIS)
1800 K St. NW, Ste. 400, Washington, DC 20006
(202) 887-0200 • fax: (202) 775-3199
website: www.csis.org

The center works to provide world leaders with strategic insights and policy options on current and emerging global issues. Numerous reports related to the war in Afghanistan can be downloaded from its website.

Council on Foreign Relations

58 E. Sixty-Eighth St., New York, NY 10021

(212) 434-9400 • fax: (212) 434-9800

e-mail: communications@cfr.org

website: www.cfr.org

The council researches the international aspects of American economic and political policies. Its journal *Foreign Affairs,* published five times a year, provides analysis on global conflicts, including the one ongoing in Afghanistan.

Foreign Policy Research Institute

1528 Walnut St., Ste. 610

Philadelphia, PA 19102

(215) 732-3774

e-mail: fpri@fpri.org

website: www.fpri.org

This nonprofit policy organization researches policy issues and publishes books, briefs, and reports on a wide variety of topics, including the Taliban and Afghanistan. Thought-provoking commentary is also found in its quarterly published journal, *Orbis.*

Hoover Institution

Stanford University, Stanford, CA 94305-6010

(650) 723-1754 • fax: (650) 723-1687

website: www.hoover.org

The Hoover Institution is a public policy research center devoted to advanced study of politics, economics, and political economy—both domestic and foreign—as well as international affairs. It publishes the quarterly *Hoover Digest,* which often includes articles on Afghanistan and the war on terrorism, as well as a newsletter, special reports, and other journals, such as *Policy Review.*

Human Rights Watch (HRW)

485 Fifth Ave., New York, NY 10017-6104

(212) 972-8400 • fax: (212) 972-0905

e-mail: hrwnyc@hrw.org

website: www.hrw.org

Human Rights Watch regularly investigates human rights abuses in over seventy countries around the world. It promotes civil liberties and defends freedom of thought, due process, and the equal protection of the law. Its goal is to hold governments accountable for human rights violations they commit against individuals because of their political, ethnic, or religious affiliations. HTW publishes a wealth of information about Afghanistan, including current information, background information, and regular human rights reports.

The National Endowment for Democracy (NED)

1101 Fifteenth St. NW, Ste. 700
Washington DC 20005
(202) 293-9072 • fax: (202) 223-6042
e-mail: info@ned.org
website: www.ned.org

NED is a private nonprofit organization created in 1983 to strengthen democratic institutions around the world through nongovernmental efforts. It publishes the bimonthly *Journal of Democracy*.

North Atlantic Treaty Organization (NATO)
International Security Assistance Force (ISAF)

Blvd. Leopold III
1110 Brussels, Belgium
website: www.nato.int/ISAF

NATO is an alliance of twenty-eight countries from North America and Europe committed to fulfilling the goals of the North Atlantic Treaty, which was signed in 1949. NATO offers a forum for member countries to consult on pressing security issues around the world and take joint action in addressing them. NATO operates the International Security Assistance Force (ISAF), the body of coalition troops in Afghanistan.

Revolutionary Association of the Women of Afghanistan (RAWA)

PO Box 374
Quetta, Pakistan
e-mail: rawa@rawa.org
website: www.rawa.org

RAWA was established in Kabul, Afghanistan, in 1977 as an independent political/social organization of Afghan women fighting for human rights and for social justice in Afghanistan. RAWA continues to fight for freedom, democracy, and women's rights in Afghanistan. It is the publisher of a bilingual (Persian/Pashtu) magazine *Payam-e-Zan,* which means "Woman's Message." Its website contains news updates and other information pertaining to women's rights in Afghanistan.

UN Development Programme (UNDP) in Afghanistan
1 United Nations Plaza, New York, NY 10017
(212) 906-5317
website: www.undp.org.af

UNDP is the United Nations' global development network, helping countries build solutions to the challenges of democratic governance, poverty reduction, crisis prevention and recovery, energy and environment, information and communications technology, and HIV/AIDS. UNDP has been present in Afghanistan for more than fifty years and works to support the people of Afghanistan as they face new challenges and move their country forward.

US Department of State
2201 C St. NW
Washington, DC 20520
(202) 647-6575
website: www.state.gov

This cabinet-level federal government agency is responsible for international relations. Its website contains a wealth of official information relating to the American relationship with Afghanistan leaders and how together they both address issues raised by the Taliban.

For Further Reading

Books

Danes, Kay. *Beneath the Pale Blue Burqa: One Woman's Journey Through Taliban Strongholds*. Newport, NSW, Australia: Big Sky, 2010. A woman describes her adventures through Taliban-held territory and the remote wastelands of al Qaeda terrorists.

Fergusson, James. *Taliban: The Unknown Enemy*. Cambridge, MA: Da Capo, 2011. A compelling account of the rise, fall, and return of the Taliban.

Jones, Seth G. *In the Graveyard of Empires: America's War in Afghanistan*. New York: Norton, 2010. This book, by a political scientist, sheds light on why Pakistan, which consistently supports the Taliban, continues to be a key player in the region's future.

Peters, Gretchen. *Seeds of Terror: How Heroin Is Bankrolling the Taliban and al Qaeda*. New York: St. Martin's, 2009. Based on hundreds of interviews with Taliban fighters, smugglers, and law enforcement and intelligence agents, this book explores how money from the drug trade keeps the Taliban and al Qaeda operating.

Shahzad, Syed Saleem. *Inside al-Qaeda and the Taliban: Beyond Bin Laden and 9/11*. London: Pluto, 2011. Introduces and examines the new generation of al Qaeda leaders who have been behind the most recent attacks.

Zaeef, Abdul Salam. *My Life with the Taliban*. New York: Columbia University Press, 2010. The memoirs of a former senior Taliban member.

Periodicals and Internet Sources

Bolton, John. "The Taliban's Atomic Threat," *Wall Street Journal*, May 2, 2009. http://online.wsj.com/article/SB124121967978578985 .html.

Bright, Arthur. "Who Are the Taliban and What Do They Want?," *Christian Science Monitor*, April 9, 2012. www.csmonitor.com /World/Asia-South-Central/2012/0409/Who-are-the-Taliban -and-what-do-they-want-5-key-points/Afghan-insurgents.

Bryen, Shoshana. "The Taliban and the PLO," *American Thinker*, January 10, 2012. www.americanthinker.com/2012/01/the_tali ban_and_the_plo.html.

Cavendish, Julius. "Why the Afghan Plan to Woo Taliban Fighters Is Floundering," *Time*, September 27, 2011. www.time.com/time /world/article/0,8599,2094897,00.html.

Coll, Steve. "Looking for Mullah Omar: Will the United States Be Able to Negotiate with a Man It Has Hunted for a Decade?," *New Yorker*, January 23, 2012. www.newyorker.com/reporting /2012/01/23/120123fa_fact_coll.

Davis, Daniel L. "Truth, Lies, and Afghanistan: How Military Leaders Have Let Us Down," *Armed Forces Journal*, February 2012. www .armedforcesjournal.com/2012/02/8904030.

Dongen, Teun van. "Why Negotiating with the Taliban Is a Really Bad Idea," *National Interest*, July 27, 2011. http://national interest.org/commentary/why-negotiating-the-taliban-really-bad -idea-5666.

Fowler, Michael. "Heroin Fix Drives Taliban," *Reflections*, December 2009. www.ebireflections.com/1/11/01_foreign_affairs.xhtml.

Glavin, Terry. "Lies, Damn Lies and the CIA's Creation of the Taliban," *National Post*, September 26, 2011. http://fullcomment .nationalpost.com/2011/09/26/terry-glavin-lies-damn-lies-and-the -cias-creation-of-the-taliban/.

Guntzel, Jeff Severns. "Who Are the Taliban and What Do They Want?," *Utne Reader*, May 26, 2009. www.utne.com/Politics/Who -are-the-Taliban-and-What-do-they-Want-Guntzel.aspx.

Hadley, Stephen, and John Podesta. "Enough Already: It's Time to Talk to the Taliban," *Foreign Policy*, January 18, 2012. www.for eignpolicy.com/articles/2012/01/18/enough_already.

Hornberger, Jacob G. "U.S. Foreign Policy Caused the Taliban Problem," Future of Freedom Foundation, May 8, 2009. www .fff.org/comment/com0905c.asp.

Hughes, John. "Obama Must Not Let Taliban Rule Over Afghan Women Again," *Christian Science Monitor*, September 8, 2010. www.csmonitor.com/Commentary/John-Hughes/2010/0908 /Obama-must-not-let-Taliban-rule-over-Afghan-women-again.

Kayyem, Juliette. "How the US Funds the Taliban," *Boston Globe*, September 19, 2011. http://articles.boston.com/2011-09-19/bostonglobe/30176732_1_afghan-national-police-afghans-first-insurgents.

Longbottom, Wil. "Turning Their Back on Violence: Taliban Insurgents Hand Over Scores of Weapons as They Try to Rejoin Society," *Daily Mail* (London), January 17, 2012. www.dailymail.co.uk/news/article-2087706/Turning-violence-Taliban-insurgents-hand-scores-weapons-try-rejoin-society.html.

Menon, Rajan. "Talking to the Taliban," *Newsday*, January 12, 2012. www.newsday.com/opinion/oped/menon-talking-to-the-taliban-1.3442781.

Moncrieff, Virginia M. "Obama's Winning Move: Negotiate with the Taliban," September 3, 2011. www.huffingtonpost.com/virginia-moncrieff/obamas-winning-move-negot_b_946042.html.

Moran, Rick. "Clearing the Way for the Taliban," *FrontPage Magazine*, April 9, 2012. http://frontpagemag.com/2012/04/09/clearing-the-way-for-the-taliban/1/.

Peters, Gretchen, interviewed by Dave Davies. "Heroin, the Taliban, and the 'Seeds of Terror,'" National Public Radio, May 11, 2009. www.npr.org/templates/transcript/transcript.php?storyId=103957098.

Posner, Gerald. "The Taliban's Nuclear Threat," Daily Beast, April 22, 2009. www.thedailybeast.com/articles/2009/04/22/the-talibans-nuclear-threat.html.

Rayment, Sean. "The Drive to Turn the Taliban to Peace," *Sunday Telegraph* (London), March 11, 2012. www.telegraph.co.uk/news/worldnews/asia/afghanistan/9135863/The-drive-to-turn-the-Taliban-to-peace.html.

Rohde, David. "Held by the Taliban," *New York Times*, October 18, 2009. www.nytimes.com/2009/10/18/world/asia/18hostage.html?pagewanted=all.

Rubin, Michael. "Talking with the Taliban Is Not Diplomacy, It's Deadly," American Enterprise Institute, September 6, 2011. www.aei.org/article/foreign-and-defense-policy/defense/talking-with-the-taliban-is-not-diplomacy-its-deadly/.

Saleh, Amrullah. "Afghan Role for Taliban, If They Play by Rules," Bloomberg, June 16, 2011. www.bloomberg.com/news/2011-06

-16/afghan-role-for-taliban-if-they-play-by-rules-amrullah-saleh
.html.

Sarwary, Bilal. "Why Taliban Are So Strong in Afghanistan,"
BBC.com, February 12, 2012. www.bbc.co.uk/news/world
-asia-16851949.

Schanzer, Jonathan. "Say It Out Loud: The Taliban Are Terrorists,"
Jewish Policy Center, March 27, 2009. www.jewishpolicycenter
.org/881/say-it-out-loud-the-taliban-are-terrorists.

Servatius, Tara. "Untold Outrage: Obama's Servile Negotiations with
the Taliban over Afghanistan," *Human Events*, June 5, 2011. www
.humanevents.com/article.php?id=43937.

Serwer, Daniel. "Why It's Time to Negotiate with the Taliban,"
Atlantic, April 7, 2011. www.theatlantic.com/international
/archive/2011/04/why-its-time-to-negotiate-with-the-taliban
/73379/.

Smith, Jordan Michael. "Rethinking the Taliban," *Salon*, January
19, 2012. www.salon.com/2012/01/19/how_to_think_about_the
_taliban/.

Taylor, Rob. "Military Comeback a Distant Dream for Afghan Taliban,"
Reuters, February 5, 2012. www.reuters.com/article/2012/02/05
/us-afganistan-taliban-military-idUSTRE81404K20120205.

Thiessen, Marc A. "Don't Let These Taliban Leaders Loose,"
Washington Post, January 9, 2012. www.washingtonpost.com/
opinions/dont-let-these-taliban-leaders-loose/2012/01/09/gIQAe
LIWlP_story.html.

Tomsen, Peter. "The Afghanistan Equation: U.S. + Taliban + Pakistan
= Peace?," *Los Angeles Times*, February 8, 2012. http://articles
.latimes.com/2012/feb/08/opinion/la-oe-0208-tomsen-afghani
stan-20120208.

Trofimov, Yaroslav. "Emboldened Taliban Try to Sell Softer Image,"
Wall Street Journal, January 28, 2012. http://online.wsj.com/arti
cle/SB10001424052970203806504577177074111336352.html.

Williamson, Kevin D. "The Taliban's Mob Rules," *National Review*,
February 21, 2012. www.nationalreview.com/articles/291512
/taliban-s-mob-rules-kevin-d-williamson.

Websites

Afghanistan News Center (www.afghanistannewscenter.com/). A collection of news related to Afghanistan from a wide variety of major news sources that is updated regularly throughout the day.

Al Jazeera (www.aljazeera.com). This international news organization is based in the Middle East and offers commentary on the Taliban (and many other topics) from a unique, non-Western perspective.

CIA World Factbook—Afghanistan Page (www.cia.gov/library /publications/the-world-factbook/geos/af.html). This site, maintained by the CIA, contains up-to-date demographic information on most nations, including Afghanistan. Students will find its maps and facts useful when doing reports and papers on this topic.

Institute for Afghan Studies (www.institute-for-afghan-studies .org). This site features commentary on the Taliban and Afghanistan from young Afghan scholars who are located all over the world.

Index

Picture Credits

© AP Images/B.K. Bangash, 39

© AP Images/U.S. Army Major James D. Crawford, 101

© AP Images/Jerome Delay, 53

© AP Images/Ishitaq Mahsud, 11

© AP Images/Anjum Naveed, 111

© AP Images/Musadeq Sadeq, 98

© Bob Collier/PA Photos/Landov, 35

© Gale/Cengage, 17, 23, 27, 36, 41, 56, 71, 76, 82, 91, 103, 108

© Andrya Hill/UPI/Landov, 29

© Massoud Hossaini/AFP/Getty Images, 84

© Ahmad Masood/Reuters/Landov, 64, 68, 86

© Ahmad Massoud/Xinhua/Landov, 78

© Reuters/Inter Services Public Relations/Landov, 48

© Reuters/Ahmad Sear/Landov, 50

© Roger L. Wollenberg/UPI/Landov, 14, 21